The Crown Colonies Of Great Britain, An Inquiry Into Their Political Economy, Fiscal System And Trade...

Charles Spencer Salmon

225

THE CROWN COLONIES

OF

GREAT BRITAIN.

An Inquiry into their Political Economy,
Fiscal Systems, and Trade.

BY

C. S. SALMON.

CASSELL & COMPANY, LIMITED:

LONDON, PARIS, NEW YORK & MELBOURNE.

COBDEN CLUB LEAFLETS.

Supplied in Packets of 100, *price* 1s.   *Those marked * * 2s.*

Cassell & Company, Limited; London, Paris, New York and Melbourne.

THE CROWN COLONIES

OF

GREAT BRITAIN.

THE CROWN COLONIES

OF

GREAT BRITAIN.

*AN INQUIRY INTO THEIR POLITICAL ECONOMY,
FISCAL SYSTEMS, AND TRADE.*

BY

C. S. SALMON.

CASSELL & COMPANY, Limited:
LONDON, PARIS, NEW YORK & MELBOURNE.

CONTENTS.

——◦◦•——

A

CONTENTS.

THE CROWN COLONIES

OF

GREAT BRITAIN.

———◆———

INTRODUCTION.

IT is right that the Crown colonies should be investigated from the statistical point of view, and should yield information that will be of use for trade purposes. What are the imports? What are the exports? How much revenue is raised? How stand the public debts? At what rate are railways being pushed forward? Does the population rapidly increase? Let us know whether it is profitable to invest in the land? And so on. Yet it is well to pause sometimes and to inquire also about the people; are they really happy and progressive in those things which make life worthy, pleasant, or even endurable to the poor; and do matters look as if a happy and estimable future lay before all or any of them? In dealing with Crown colonies people at home are apt to take a very narrow and material view indeed, deliberately or unconsciously. And yet these colonies, even the smaller ones, are countries often as large and as full of people as many a place in Europe which holds a niche of its own in the world's history, and whose movements are watched and recorded by the public press of the world. These latter countries, however small they may be, are important as the homes of a people who are, or have been, factors in the political and social questions of the day. Of imports there may be none beyond those necessary for the civilised wants of a frugal race, and the exports may be equally unnoticeable, because the people are of more importance than the productions they have to dispose of. With the Crown colonies it is different; they are apt to be written and spoken of as if their productions, actual or potential, were of more importance than

A 2

the inhabitants; and yet it is a fact that imports and exports, and revenue and debts, and population, may all show an increase, and the condition of the people may not be advanced, or may even have retrograded amidst all this show.

With the above reservations, the value of colonies has never been underrated by the people of the United Kingdom; no party ever existed in this country, in recent times, which had not the highest opinion, at all events, of their practical worth and of their commercial necessity. The people of Great Britain and Ireland have made immense sacrifices in the past to obtain and protect the colonies of the empire; for upwards of a century their acquisition and consolidation has been one of the objects of every popular administration, and their life has become a part of the social and industrial life of the people of the United Kingdom. Yet there are those who seem to think it quite a new and recent movement for the people of these islands to be interested in colonial questions. It may be so with certain classes of the community, whose natural sympathies and habits would have had little in common with the first struggling communities of settlers in what are now the free colonies. But since then these colonies have grown to be rich and powerful, and the fruits of labour, industry, and intelligence are abundant, and hence a sympathy among the highest classes in the land has arisen, which before lay somewhat dormant. The bulk of the people, however, are connected with the great colonies by ties of a nearer and more enduring nature, and without show and ostentation, and unknown even to their own rulers, they have always looked on them as a part of the United Kingdom, and as the inalienable inheritance of their race.

The Crown colonies are distinguished at once from the free parliamentary colonies inhabited by European races, in that they are apt to be handed over by the consent of all parties in power, and also by the public opinion of the country, to the guidance and even control of those classes and interests which have immediate dealings with them; and hence the people who inhabit them, outside of these classes, receive less sympathy and consideration from the people of the United Kingdom than they are entitled to. They have, undoubtedly, all been given systems of administration they would perhaps have in vain looked for from any other nation in a kind of liberality of government and, in particular instances, even in some power of self-development. Yet something more is needed, if not to insure prosperity and comfort to the people, at least not to hinder its establishment, its endurance, or its advance. By the side of those forms of government which secure the impartiality of criminal and civil law, and those systems of administration which make its enforcement equal for all, there are certain laws and systems which affect the material welfare of society, and which are more powerful in their operations than any other agencies established among men. The methods of taxation, and the systems regulating and affecting trade, and the laws dealing with the acquisition and the working of land and other property, may be equal for all who come within their scope and operation, and, nevertheless, they may all be so adjusted as to militate against the most elementary principles of right upon which the welfare of a community must be founded in order to thrive. They may work so as to favour monopolies. Burdens, also, may fall on certain classes whilst others are exempted. In fact, the system of government may be a just one, politically and legally, and the most suitable and the best procurable, theoretically, under the circumstances of the colony, and the administration of the existing laws may be admirable and impartial, and yet many evils may accumulate because the economic systems in operation contain within themselves elements of evil which are bound to bear evil fruit.

All this is so obvious to those acquainted with these colonies that it gives rise to a conviction in many minds that the only people fit to judge of internal affairs in any country whatever are the people who inhabit it. On the other hand, the mixed communities of races, with opposite views and often hostile interests, which inhabit some of the Crown colonies, make the full application of such views impracticable at present, or extremely difficult. It remains only for absolute justice to be dealt out to all classes equally, irrespective of race and interest.

There is a tendency among all men to form exclusive societies, but the least civilised people are the most exclusive in their views, and they desire to have but little intercourse with other races. Some Englishmen have objected to the extended views of those of their fellow-countrymen who deem the interests of other races and countries are allied to their own—men whose general opinions have made them almost as much citizens of the world at large as of their own particular land—because they feared such views tended to disarm or deaden that feeling of

patriotism which is essential to the preservation of the position of their own country. But it is obvious that a great commercial and colonial country must have these cosmopolitan and less exclusive views, or its success and continuance as a centre of enterprise will not be possible. The greater success of England as a colonial and commercial power over other nations has been due to the greater respect she has, on the whole, always shown for rights she deems fundamental, and due to all mankind; and especially for the rights and welfare of those weaker races which circumstances have placed under her power and control. The greatest force in the world is man, and the more that is learned respecting him, the more it is seen that the several varieties have much in common, and that the differences so well known and so often deplored are not due to anything more than dissimilar physical and moral surroundings working throughout the ages. To deal successfully with the tropical jungles of Crown colonies, and to cultivate their heated plains, the races accustomed to the climate and inured to the toil are required, and where these fail nothing can be done. To get due value from these countries, and to develop their wealth in a solid form, the men inhabiting them must be encouraged to bear a willing hand by reaping the just reward of labour; sufficient inducements must be given them to struggle upwards to a higher standard. Stagnation or a falling away can be generally traced to a state of things which disorganises local industry. The reward of labour must leave some fair margin beyond the scanty necessities of a mere existence, or, in tropical countries at all events, it will be found the inhabitants will abandon regular work and relapse into those primitive conditions from which it is the duty of civilised and orderly Government to make efforts to reclaim them. As far back as 1824 the Report of the Parliamentary Committee on labourers' wages said:—
"He, whose subsistence is secure without work, and who cannot obtain more than a mere sufficiency by the hardest work, will naturally be an idle and careless labourer." The past economic history of many of the Crown colonies may be summarised as constant endeavours to struggle against these facts and natural laws in favour of the planting and absentee interests, efforts fruitful of calamities to the colonies and to their inhabitants.

With respect to the public opinion of the Crown colonies, it is undeniably a power which in recent times is making itself more and more felt. The press in many of them has organs conducted with ability, and in some of them with singular power and conspicuous fairness; the proprietors and editors are not confined to any one race, and no one could proclaim from internal evidence the nationality of a writer. But the wants and rights of the majority of the people are not always represented in the columns of the public press in the Crown colonies, and this makes it the more necessary for the people and Parliament of the United Kingdom to pay some attention to what is passing, for they are undoubtedly responsible for the laws and systems upheld in these dependencies.

The tariff questions especially are very important, for it can be proved that the methods pursued—which date from the time of protectionist and anti-free trade policy—have been adverse to the best interests of the United Kingdom, and have hampered the development of her trade with the colonies; while, at the same time, they have been injurious to the welfare, the comfort, and the happiness of the colonists themselves. So many anti-free trade centres of commerce dispersed all over the world under the British flag have, beyond all doubt, had a most injurious effect, and have obstructed and hindered the propagation of free trade principles among the nations. Even in those colonies now possessing responsible governments the restrictive tariffs which British merchants and manufacturers so much complain of are no worse than some of those set up in certain Crown colonies to their disadvantage, and, in fact, such tariffs are often, to some extent, the legacy the Parliamentary colonies received over from the periods when they were under the direct administration of the Crown.

In a paper, which received much attention not only from every colonist, but from every person interested in colonial questions, contributed to the "Nineteenth Century Review"* by the Right Honourable W. E. Forster, M.P., it is said :—" I do not think we can expect newly formed communities to raise their revenue solely by direct taxation, but the abolition of all custom or excise, except upon intoxicating liquors and tobacco, and the general equalisation of these taxes, would make an Imperial Zollverein possible." The necessities of none of the Crown colonies require more than what is succinctly laid down here. Professor J. E. Thorold Rogers,

* February, 1885.

M.P., in his work, "Six Centuries of Work and Wages," also says (Vol. I., page 212):—"It is always difficult to raise a revenue from direct taxation in a country where industry is mainly agricultural;" but, of course, the Professor—who says elsewhere, "to tax what a man must spend is to destroy industry"—means a moderate tax, and on commodities such as Mr. Forster mentions. Mr. Leroy-Beaulieu is an admirer of the colonial capacities of Englishmen; he says that a customs charge—never imposed for protectionist purposes, and never exceeding 5 per cent. *ad valorem*—and land revenues, are the only proper colonial taxes except those on spirits and tobacco, articles which should be charged more heavily. He goes on to say that these are the only taxes universally applied (as he describes them) in the British colonies with no ill result, and giving sufficient revenues. Most Englishmen who know the colonies will admit this statement gives a fair outline of the system that might be followed, but is not. Mr. Leroy-Beaulieu had probably in view, when he wrote the above, a proposition made about that time to put into practice the system he eulogises.

The population of the twelve groups of Crown colonies (Gibraltar, Malta, Ceylon, Mauritius, Straits Settlements, Hong Kong, Fiji, Falkland Islands, the West Indian Islands and Mainland, Bermuda, St. Helena, and Western Coast of Africa), at the close of 1883, amounted to about 6,504,200. The revenues raised in 1883 amounted to £6,577,226. The public debts for the whole equalled £6,000,000. The Straits Settlements—especially Singapore—Hong Kong, Gibraltar, and Malta, are ports of call and entrepôts, whose returns (when given) of total imports and exports have more reference to the trade of neighbouring and distant foreign countries with Great Britain and other nations than to the trade done within such colonies themselves. Excluding these four colonies, therefore, the total imports of the other eight groups of colonies, in 1883, amounted to £18,823,278, and their total exports were £19,430,504 (colonial returns). Of the imports the sum of £5,822,800 (Board of Trade returns) represents the value of the produce and manufactures of the United Kingdom, or about 31 per cent. The exports from these colonies to the United Kingdom direct were valued (Board of Trade returns) at £8,608,212, or about 45¼ per cent. of the whole. The total trade of these colonies for the year 1883 amounted to

£38,253,782 (colonial returns), of which £14,431,012 (Board of Trade returns) was with the United Kingdom, or nearly 38 per cent. of the whole.

There are no returns whatever to be had respecting imports and exports at the ports of Hong Kong and Gibraltar. The Straits Settlements and Malta between them have £41,558,644 imports, and £40,736,029 exports, for the year 1883. The figures for Hong Kong and Gibraltar would probably be as much as this. As a matter of fact, such returns from these ports often only repeat one another; the same vessel, with the identical cargo on board, will sometimes enter at all of them on a single voyage, and, after coaling and discharging some cargo, clear outwards, and proceed with the remainder. The Board of Trade returns for the year 1883 show exports from the United Kingdom of British goods, for Gibraltar and Malta direct, amounting to £1,712,653, and imports therefrom to the value of £190,789. The great free trade ports of the East—the Straits Settlements and Hong Kong—took British merchandise valued by Board of Trade returns at £5,515,478, and sent produce valued at £5,815,002 to the United Kingdom.

It will be seen that the trade of the Crown colonies is large, but, except with the great free trade Eastern ports, it is not by a long way as large as it might be. The system of tariffs—as in the West Indies, Ceylon, Mauritius, Fiji, and Malta—and the general policy pursued with regard to the natives—as in Western Africa—have much hindered material progress, and these colonies do not compare as favourably as they ought to with the colonies of foreign powers, where the policy pursued is not pretended to be entirely—if at all—in the interest of the inhabitants. Indeed, the position of the people in many of these Crown colonies is unsatisfactory, for reasons that will be shown farther on, when the colonies are separately dealt with. The taxation per head paid by the people of a colony is no more a criterion by which to form any judgment respecting it than the exports alone can be taken as a basis on which to build up a theory of the people's wealth, prosperity, and happiness. A man can better afford to save 10s. in Australasia than a Cingalese can afford to save 4d. The West India colonies export at the rate of £6 12s. per inhabitant (nearly the same rate as for the United Kingdom), and pay Government taxes at the rate of 26s. 6d. only; and yet the bulk of the people, as regards housing, food, and the

common necessaries of a civilised life, are worse off than the
serfs of the Middle Ages.   Can they be compared for an instant
with the great colony of the Cape of Good Hope, whose
people export only at the rate of 70s. 5d. per head, and yet pay
taxes at the rate of 87s. 1d. per head? or with the savage but
vigorous natives of their own Africa?   At the same time, it is
a sound criterion to take the exports of a colony, if the wealth
raised and exported be really raised and owned by the people.
The twenty and a half millions sterling of exports from Canada
in 1883 were undoubtedly, nearly all of them, the property of
the Canadians themselves, and almost the whole proceeds of
profits went to enrich the inhabitants.   In the West Indies
and other tropical colonies the people, owing to various
reasons, have not the capital necessary to accomplish that
work which people in more happily formed societies are
expected to do for themselves.   Extraneous aid from foreign
capitalists is sometimes sought by, and sometimes forced on, the
people of tropical countries, to assist them to cultivate their
lands.   Nothing is more certain than that this capital, in
whatever form it comes, can permanently develop the wealth
of the several colonies, because, as Professor Leone Levi says
("History of British Commerce," p. 149), "there is one un-
alterable law as regards wages : they depend on capital.
However fertile the soil, however favourable the position of
the country, however great the extent of territory, unless there
be sufficient capital in hand to maintain labour, nothing can be
done."   But this capital can only do good permanently on
condition the other elements employed in the work also
receive a fair share of the profits.   The wages of labour, in
every instance, can be left to be settled between the employer
and the employed ; and where there are no inhabitants in an
annexed territory, it is legitimate enough to seek for people in
other countries.   But the Government does not stop at this ;
and if there is labour to be had on the spot, but the labourer
sulks at the terms offered by planters and capitalists, starveling
coolies from India are sent to replace it, and the wages of
labour in that colony are forced down to the lowest limits that
admit of a bare existence.   Taxation, also, forced from its
natural channels by the exigencies of a system which has
allowed predominance to absentees and their agents, has fallen
almost entirely on the struggling labourers.   In course of time
a system, symmetrical in all its parts, has arisen on this basis.

It is correct in its law and perfect in its constitutionalism; but it wants one thing—a people able to live contentedly and thrive by the sweat of its brow. Systems are worthless that do not create such men. Capital accumulates among the people in such places with extreme difficulty, because there is no margin left for the reward of thrift.

The keeping of order and the protection of private rights constitute the main work of Government, but the people have other wants with which a Government should have no concern, and when it does enter the lists monopolies and abuses grow up and abound, unless strict watch be kept; the Government after a time loses control over the instruments it has set up, and opposite results come about from those avowedly intended. The Crown colonies are full of such instances. The introduction of coolie labour into colonies where it may have been supposed to be wanted was doubtless at the beginning a well-intentioned act; the abuses that have since arisen might have been foreseen, but were not. Englishmen should not be behind foreigners in appreciating what is just. This is what Mr. Leroy-Beaulieu says on the subject:—" Cette immigration, au point de vue social, quand elle porte sur les Chinois ou sur les Indiens, a les plus déplorables résultats; ces hommes appartenant, non pas à des sociétés primitives dont les membres sont prêts à se fondre par un instinct naturel dans les sociétés plus avancées, mais à des sociétés vieilles et décrépites, conservant avec ténacité leurs habitudes et leurs moeurs." They keep also their language and their religion; having few females among them, the deplorable results to the places they are sent to are well known and are repugnant to every social sentiment. Again he says:—" Au point de vue économique, les conséquences ne sont pas moins fatales. C'est la facilité de l'immigration, qui, en partie, a été la cause de l'abandon définitif des habitations par les noirs; les planteurs n'ont plus songé à les retenir par de bons traitements et des égards" . . . "le second inconvénient économique de l'immigration, c'est qu'elle détourne les colons des améliorations nécessaires qui, en utilisant mieux le nombre de bras existants, et en perfectionnant les procédés, multiplieraient considérablement les quantités produites et le revenu net."* With refer-

---

* There have been rumours that a new coolie colony was to be created in Northern Queensland by the introduction of that form of servile labour. It is to be hoped free Australia will keep such a thing from its shores.

ence to labour in tropical Crown colonies generally, it is needful to draw public attention to the large employment of woman labour in that most trying of all labour—working in a cane field.   This class of labour is very cheap, but it is disastrous to the community.   In his work, "The State in Relation to Labour," the late Mr. Stanley Jevons said (p. 70), on the employment of mothers :—"The great evil which arises from such employment is the separation of the mother from her young children ; in the case of infants who ought to be suckled the result is usually disastrous . . . a large proportion succumb, and those who by any fortunate accident of more vigorous constitution, or slightly better treatment, survive, are too often ruined physically and mentally, and grow up into a stunted and sickly generation."   He shows how the German Social Science Association and the statistics of the United States Agricultural Bureaus fully support these views.   After long fasting on the part of mother and infant, when at last the latter obtains the breast, the mother's body is heated and exhausted, and the worst results follow for the infant.   In all the West India colonies especially, but particularly so in some of them, the enormous proportions of this evil are quite startling.

A good deal has yet to be done to perfect cultivation in many colonies, especially with regard to sugar.   Immense advances have been made in Europe in recent years in the cultivation and preparation of beet sugar, and the severe competition that has arisen in the sugar markets has been due more to this than to the bounties.   The fall in the price of sugar will not be entirely without compensation ; it has caused it to enter into many industries, from which, in the future, it will be inseparable.   From time to time, it is to be feared, blights will do more damage to colonial produce than competition ; the coffee growers of Ceylon found this to be the case.   An acre of land may yield a ton of beetroot sugar in three years.   An acre of virgin soil gives $1\frac{1}{2}$ ton of cane sugar ; most of the British sugar colonies give over $1\frac{1}{4}$ ton an acre.   They should do better than the beet growers even with their bounties.   If all the projects on foot to grow sugar in tropical colonies were to succeed, there would be some difficulty in disposing of the supply.   The British sugar colonies would be thriving now if their economical and fiscal systems were not deplorably unsound.   It wanted the fall in the price of sugar to demonstrate beyond question this unsoundness, and it is quite certain nothing can place these colonies on the road to prosperity and stability but a commercial and economical system entirely different from that under which they now have to struggle. Free trade in land and in commerce and the tariffs of Mr. Forster quoted above, are the chief remedies wanted.

The colonies take a good deal of merchandise from foreign countries, as much in proportion to their general trade as the United Kingdom does; they have many wants foreign countries alone can supply. Those who urge a customs union between the colonies and the United Kingdom, on the basis of either party taking the produce of another, with differential tariffs against foreigners, will have many interests to deal with and to consider that are hostile to such proposals. There are some things the colonies produce for which they find advantageous markets abroad, and they are rather anxious to increase this commerce than to diminish it. Those colonies which produce wine will want the people of the United Kingdom to continue to drink it, because it does not sell so readily abroad, but for their part they will take for their own use much of the vintages of the Rhine and Bordeaux, and pay for it, if they can, in their own productions. As in the past, so in the future, those people will do the most trade who give the best and cheapest articles that may be wanted, and success will eventually depend on skill, energy, enterprise, and the highest intelligence. The parliamentary colonies are mostly (for the present) so elated over protection, which they appear rich enough to be able to bear, that any arrangement with the United Kingdom, tending to remove her free trade policy, will probably be pleasing to them, especially if it raises the price of any of their produce in British markets; if it does not do this they will not care for it, but they will not object to it, it will really matter so very little to them. It is pretty certain they will make no convention which will in any way damage their trade prospects with other countries. The great colonies are in the position to gain, whatever policy Great Britain, or indeed any other country, may follow.

Every one knows how the value of land has fallen in England; in France the fall has been 40 per cent. in some places, and a man is deemed lucky who makes $2\frac{1}{2}$ per cent. out of it in that country from corn growing. Neither free trade England, by conventions with Canada and Australasia, nor protectionist France, by high duties, can cause this economical result to be reversed. If the value of land falls in the old countries, it rises in the new ones ; it is only cause and effect. In the tropical colonies also, competition is intense, and, as a virgin soil accessible to labour can produce some crops 30 per cent. cheaper than the wearied soil of older colonies, the latter, like England and France, have to turn their hands to producing those other crops which the circumstances of the markets make profitable.

If any fair trade or reciprocal treaty tariffs are proposed to be imposed in the United Kingdom, it is only right it should be known at once that it will not be in the interests of the colonies that it will be done, but solely in the interests of those at home who desire protection, and whose private interests never allowed them to be really convinced that free trade was beneficial to the United Kingdom.

CHAPTER I.

THE WEST INDIES.

In Professor Leone Levi's work ("History of British Commerce"), on comparing the returns for the year 1850 with those for 1877, the following results are given. The total general trade of the West India Islands had increased in value during that interval by 177 per cent., but their trade with the United Kingdom had diminished in value by 9 per cent.; in the former year the United Kingdom did 68 per cent. of the trade and only 34 per cent. of it in the latter year. The total trade of British Guiana had increased during the 28 years by 227 per cent., and the trade of the United Kingdom with the colony had increased by 55 per cent. during the same period; but the percentage of this colony's trade with the United Kingdom had fallen from 78 per cent. of the whole in 1850 to 37 per cent. of the whole in 1877.

Taking all the West India colonies, the total exports for the six years ending 1871 were about 45 millions sterling, of which the United Kingdom received $31\frac{1}{4}$ millions. For the six years ending 1877 there were over $49\frac{1}{2}$ millions exports, of which the United Kingdom received under $34\frac{1}{2}$ millions. For the six years ending 1883 the exports exceeded $55\frac{1}{2}$ millions, of which the United Kingdom received $34\frac{1}{4}$ millions.

The imports into the West India colonies for the six years ending 1871 were about 38 millions sterling, of which the United Kingdom sent $17\frac{1}{2}$ millions. For the six years ending 1877 they were about 45 millions, of which the United Kingdom sent a little over $20\frac{1}{2}$ millions. For the six years ending 1883 they were nearly $51\frac{1}{4}$ millions, of which the United Kingdom sent under 21 millions.

It thus appears that between the years 1871 and 1877 the exports of these colonies had increased by $4\frac{1}{2}$ millions sterling, of which the United Kingdom received $3\frac{1}{3}$ millions; and between the latter year and 1883 there had been a further increase in the value of exports to the amount of 6 millions sterling, of which the United Kingdom received none. In imports the increase had been 7 millions between the years 1871 and 1877, of which the United Kingdom sent 3 millions;

and between the latter year and 1883 there had been a further
increase in imports to the extent of 6¼ millions sterling, but
the United Kingdom sent only about ⅛ million of this
increase.

During the 12 years ending 1883, about £6,632,210 in
bullion and specie (included in above figures), was imported
into the Island of Trinidad, and of this all but £1,383,258
was re-exported.* The imports of bullion and specie into the
other West India colonies for the above period are inconsiderable.

The average value of the exports from the West India
colonies to the United Kingdom has not varied to any considerable extent during the last 18 years, although the quantity
has been greater. For the 10 years ending 1875 it averaged
£5,340,000 a year, the average for the 5 years ending 1880
was about £5,917,000 a year, and for the 3 years ending 1883
£5,068,719 a year. The fall in the price of sugar partly
accounts for the falling off ·in the value of produce imported
into the United Kingdom from these colonies during late
years.

The imports from the United Kingdom into the West India
colonies (including bullion and specie, and foreign and
colonial produce and manufactures) averaged £3,135,000 a
year for the ten years ending 1875, £3,445,000 a year for the
five years ending 1880, and £3,786,000 a year for the three
years ending 1883.

The above import values of goods and specie include
freight and some charges.

In the above shipments from the United Kingdom, an
average of about £325,000 a year, for the whole period, will
be for colonial and foreign produce and manufactures, the
balance being British goods and specie.

According to Board of Trade returns, the imports into the
United Kingdom from the West India possessions averaged
£5,935,000 a year for the three years 1881–83, and the
exports thereto from the United Kingdom for the same period
averaged £3,500,000 a year. This is about 17 per cent. more
for West India imports than is given by the colonial returns,

* Much of the balance was probably taken away by the coolies leaving
Trinidad, and would not figure in any returns ; a good deal of the imported
coin will have passed through the hands of the people as wages paid and
spent, before re-exportation.

and $8\frac{1}{6}$ per cent. less for exports to the West Indies than is shown by the colonial returns. On both sides the imports are more highly valued than at the ports whence they were sent. It will be seen farther on that the differences between the colonial and Board of Trade returns in the West Indies are only about a quarter of the differences that are shown to exist in some other colonies.

In the five years ending 1877 the United States sent 47 millions dollars of goods to the British West India colonies, and in the five years ending 1882 exactly another 47 millions of dollars' worth (a total for the ten years of £19,584,000 at 4s. 2d. a dollar) mostly in flour and other provisions. In the five years ending 1877 the United States received 33 millions dollars' in produce from the British West India colonies, and in the five years ending 1882 the amount was $39\frac{1}{2}$ millions of dollars worth (a total of £15,104,000 for the ten years). During the ten years ending 1882 the United States sent to these colonies $21\frac{1}{2}$ millions dollars (about £4,479,000) more merchandise than they took in produce and other commodities. This balance was probably paid in cash or bills. In some places, as at Barbados, Americans sell their provisions for cash, and they pay cash for the produce they purchase; but for convenience of comparison it will be necessary, in colonial dealings with other countries, as well as with Great Britain, to give comparative statements, in order to demonstrate the position they hold towards one another as consumers of each other's produce and merchandise; for in the end trade depends on these results, whatever may have been the medium employed in the exchange of commodities.

During the same ten years these colonies exported £57,300,000 to the United Kingdom, and took $34\frac{1}{2}$ millions in merchandise and specie; they consequently exported to the United Kingdom £22,800,000 more in produce and other commodities than they took in merchandise and in money; so that these colonies took £14,916,000 more from the United Kingdom than from the United States, and exported £42,200,000 more to the United Kingdom than to the United States in the ten years (1873–82). The total trade with the United States for the ten years was £34,688,000, and with the United Kingdom £91,800,000.

During the same ten years (1873–82) the British West Indies imported from Cuba and the Spanish West India

B

possessions about £796,000 in merchandise, and the Spanish possessions took in return only £145,000, so that some other means of paying the balance of £65,000 a year must have been provided by the British colonies.

From British North America, the four chief colonies—Jamaica, Barbados, Trinidad, and British Guiana—during the four years ending 1881, took £1,350,000 in merchandise (chiefly provisions), and sent only £1,115,000 in produce and other forms of payment. In the two years 1882-83 they took £801,000, and sent £1,176,000. British North America has, therefore, been importing more produce, recently, from the British West Indies. Jamaica, British Guiana, and Trinidad imported to the value of £1,300,000 from India in the three years 1881-83, and as there were only £1,344 exports in return, the amount due was probably paid through London. These are the three colonies that chiefly import Indian coolies.

Trinidad does a large trade with Venezuela, importing in the ten years 1874-83, £5,099,000, and exporting £2,629,000. It would appear that some Venezuela exports find their way to European markets *via* Trinidad. This is also the only West India colony that deals considerably with France. It sent £2,076,000 of produce to that country in the five years 1879-83, receiving in return only £695,000. The balance (£1,381,000) being probably paid in cash, in bills, and through London. The produce sent to France was mostly cocoa.

The British West India colonies do a certain trade amongst themselves, but only to a limited extent; some ports in Barbados and other places are used as depôts, whence American and other stores are distributed among minor colonies.

On the whole it may be seen that the West India colonies, in their dealings with other countries (except France), usually take from them considerably more than they export to them, and that in their dealings with the United Kingdom it is the reverse; they give her more than they take. The British markets evidently continue to be the best for the sale of produce, and London being the centre of commercial transactions to most countries, accounts between foreign countries and other colonies are best settled there.

The value of apparel, cotton, linen, and woollen goods, the produce and manufacture of the United Kingdom, imported into the West India colonies in the five years 1879-83, amounted to £6,205,000, the total of United Kingdom produce and manufactures of all kinds being £15,181,000 in the five years.

It is as well to draw attention to the fact that the foreign West India colonies, that is to say, the Danish, Dutch, French and Spanish West Indies, and Haïti and San Domingo (total population of all about 3,500,000) import between them, from the United Kingdom, merchandise of the yearly value, taking an average of five years, 1879–83, of nearly £3,750,000, all of which, with the exception of about £600,000 a year in rice, for the possessions of Spain—principally from India and Burmah—were nearly exclusively British goods. This is over £368,000 a year more than the British West Indies took during the same period. The total average yearly exports to England from these foreign West Indies, for the same period, was £2,189,000. They took, in the five years, £18,722,000 in merchandise from the United Kingdom, and sent exports valued at £10,945,000. It thus appears that these countries take from the United Kingdom about £1,555,000 a year more in imports than they send her in exports. It has been seen that the United Kingdom trade with the British West Indies lies quite the other way. During the same period of five years they took only £16,909,000 imports (including specie and foreign and colonial produce and manufactures) from the United Kingdom, sending her £31,860,000 of their exports.

The total tonnage entered and cleared from all the ports of the British West Indies in the four years, 1880–83, was 12,006,047 tons for steamers, and 7,838,915 tons for sailing vessels, 15,115,795 of the whole tonnage being British. Most steamers call at every port of importance on a voyage, and many sailing vessels call at more than one port.

The following are the chief tariffs on articles imported into the West Indies. The highest are paid by the people of Jamaica. They pay 8s. for every 196 lb. of flour, or one halfpenny per lb. duty! It is not to be wondered at that the labouring population consume of this luxury only about four ounces a week per head. Most of the other West Indian colonies charge about one farthing per lb. duty, and consume a trifle more of the article. Flour foods are perishable commodities in tropical climates; they soon deteriorate in value, and are easily crowded with weevils. Money, also, commands a much higher interest in these places than in the United

B 2

Kingdom (the *lowest* rate charged for *good* paper is 6 per cent. at the chief ports). A tradesman, who has to pay the duties on flour always in cash, while the flour itself is often paid for in produce or in bills, will expect a return equal to double the amount advanced, in order to cover a possible loss by waste and deterioration. A flour duty (especially a high one) is the worst form of tax that could be imposed in the tropics ; it increases the amount of the risk of the importer to such an extent that he has to charge much more in proportion for the article than is represented by the extra cost to him, and it helps to induce him to import only such quantities as he is certain to find a ready market for. The average duty on wheaten flour in the West Indies is equal to about 26 per cent. on its first cost (flour at 16s. a barrel of 196 lb., at port of shipment or on board) at present prices of low grade flour. For the reason given above this will make it cost 39 per cent. more to the purchaser than would be the case if it were free of duty. In Jamaica, where the duty on flour is about 50 per cent. on its first cost, the effects will proportionately be more severe, and the difference to the retail purchaser will be formidable indeed. The ordinary labourer cannot afford flour food as a usual diet, if at all, on these conditions. The average cost of a pound of bread made of a low-grade flour, and more or less adulterated with the flour of manioc and other inferior and lower-priced substances, is 3d. in the West Indies. The duty on flour is only 10 per cent. *ad valorem* at Honduras, and about 22 per cent. (3s. 6d. a barrel of 196 lb.) at Trinidad.

Corn meal is moderately used, and by the labouring population only. In Jamaica it pays a quarter the amount of duty charged on flour entering that colony ; in the other colonies it pays about half the duty flour pays, the average is 16 per cent. on first cost. In Barbados and British Guiana the duties are less—about 7 per cent. to 8 per cent. on first cost. Flour is permitted to enter the little island of Montserrat free.

Rice is more generally consumed in the coolie colonies of Trinidad and British Guiana, but it is also moderately used in the other colonies. The low-priced Rangoon qualities are usually imported. Jamaica duty figures highest at 3s. per 100 lb., equal to about 41 per cent. on first cost, at 8s. per cwt. on board. Trinidad charges about 27 per cent., and

British Guiana about 13 per cent. ; Barbados charges only 6½ per cent. ; the other colonies charge from 10 per cent. to 20 per cent. duty on first cost (on board).

The duties on biscuits, grain, peas, beans, and farinaceous substances not specially referred to, are all somewhat in the same proportion to value as those above given. These are all staple articles of food, and, it is not too much to say, the more they are employed by the people, the better for all classes. A superior diet, for which a man will have to labour regularly, will improve his physical powers and increase his self-respect, and add stability to industry. It will be seen, however, that some of the tariffs are almost, if not quite, prohibitory, and others are so high as to be unjust. For those who study Blue Books, it may be well to mention that the returns they embody are often on these subjects incorrect and delusive. An article in one colony will be valued at 24s., and at another colony not fifty miles distant the same class of article will be valued, at the same time, at 38s. ; at one place a thing will be valued at 5s., and thirty miles off they will place it at 12s. Some of these figures must be incorrect. The articles so valued are often imported by the same vessel and shipped from the same port at the same time. In dealing with prices, the cost on board or at the port of shipment should be taken, which, of course, is liable to vary, and does vary, but it varies equally for all. The prices in local markets of limited extent may vary largely on the spot, for local reasons, within a few months or weeks, and it would be misleading to endeavour to follow them. Besides, the prices may be put down from the two or three parcels of a high class imported for special use, and not from the average quality with which the public get supplied. It is probable, also, that in some instances not only freight and charges are added, but even prospective profits. This would naturally cause a specific duty to look less. In dealing with *ad valorem* duties the merchant will be certain to be strict, and not to overvalue his goods to the customs authorities. *Ad valorem* duties are charged on the prices of articles at port of shipment, or nearly so. Goods paying specific duties should be valued similarly.

Fish, dry- and wet-salted, is an article of diet a good deal too much employed, perhaps, by the people, for the quality is often of the worst. Here the Blue Books are evidently misleading, for the invoice prices of the same article vary sometimes

100 per cent. in ports almost within sight of one another. It is remarkable, also, that where the duties are highest there the prices are put very high, and when the duties are comparatively low the prices are less in proportion. Now this cannot be the case in business; the greater duty will enhance the price after, not before, its payment. In Barbados these duties are comparatively low, in the other colonies they are far too high, notably in Jamaica, where the customs charges are 3s. 6d. per 100 lb. of dry fish, equal to $18\frac{1}{2}$ per cent., and 1s. 2d. to 2s. 3d. per 100 lb. wet fish, equal to 20 per cent. to 30 per cent. *ad valorem*. The other colonies vary from 1s. to 2s. for same weight. Trinidad allows these articles to enter free.

Salt meat is charged 8s., 10s., 12s. 6d. up to 15s. on a barrel of 200 lb. The first cost value will vary between 40s. and 60s., according to the nature and quality. The duty on this article therefore varies from $13\frac{1}{3}$ per cent. to $37\frac{1}{2}$ per cent. *ad valorem*, according to the port it enters at. Trinidad charges no duty on salt meat.

The duties charged on articles of secondary importance for food are usually so high that they must have the effect of restricting their importation and lessening the revenue that might be derived from them; these duties, on the whole, are sometimes higher even than those imposed by the deliberately restrictive tariffs of the neighbouring colonies of foreign powers, and are equal to those imposed by protectionist countries, who desire the articles to be shut out from their markets. Jamaica charges 2d. per lb. on cheese, butter, bacon, sausages, and hams. These articles are mainly imported from the United States, and the duty will average from 18 per cent. or 20 per cent. on butter and ham, to 40 per cent. on cheese and sausages, and 33 per cent. on bacon, on the first cost. The effect of such a heavy charge will fall on the consumer, who will have to pay about double this duty by the time the article leaves the retailer's hands. The charges in the other West India colonies on these articles average about half those of Jamaica.

There are duties on lard, soap, candles, salt, and other household articles too many to enumerate; but the amount imposed is sufficient to seriously enhance the cost of all of them to the people. There is a duty on coffee, which is probably protective, as the people may often grow their own supplies. The duty on raw sugar varies from 100 per cent. or more on its present value in some colonies through almost every stage of duty ; but on the whole it acts, as probably it was intended to act, as a prohibition to importation. The case of refined sugar is different ; this is a British manufacture, and the sugar-growing colonies, who are anxious that the United Kingdom should buy their raw sugar, put a prohibitive duty on its return in a refined condition. The average duty is from ¾d. to 1½d. per lb., which will have the effect of restricting the supply, and more than doubling the cost to the consumer. Sugar imported into the Bahamas for preserving and packing fruits is exempted from duty. The duty on tea is comparatively moderate in the West Indies, except in Jamaica, Bahamas, and Honduras, where they charge 1s. per lb. ; but it is an article not extensively used by the people.

Rum and gin are the only spirituous liquors much employed by the people. The duties on these vary in every colony. It may be said to be tolerably high in some of them, considering the intrinsic value of the article, in many it is evidently too low. It is 10s. a gallon at Jamaica, 8s. 4d. at British Guiana, 6s. to 8s. at Trinidad, 3s. to 6s. at Barbados, 3s. to 7s. at the Windward Islands, and from 1s. 6d. to 5s. in the Leeward Islands, 3s. to 9s. at Bahamas, and 9s. at Honduras. If these duties are imposed on any determined principle, the variations in amount of duty charged will show that they have not been made clear. The duties on beer average from 6d. to 1s. per doz. quarts, and in wood from 2d. to 1s. the gallon. The duty on wines differ in each colony. Some charge 15 per cent., others 20 per cent., others 25 per cent. *ad valorem*, and others 1s. to 6s., or 2s. to 8s., or 4s. to 8s. per dozen bottles specific duty, according to quality and strength ; the duty on wine in the wood varies from 15 per cent. to 25 per cent. *ad valorem*, and from 1s., 2s. 6d., or 4s. per gallon specific duty.

Tobacco may be regarded as a necessary, at least the people so regard it. The amount of duty charged varies much, and it is difficult to find a sufficient reason for this ; unmanufactured tobacco pays 6d. per lb. at Jamaica and Barbados, it pays 1s. 0½d. to 1s. 5½d. at British Guiana, and 9d. at Trinidad. At Honduras, St. Christopher, and Nevis, it is 2½d. per lb., 1½d. at Bahamas, and 3d. to 1s. elsewhere. 3d. per lb. would not be an unfair duty ; it would be equal to about 40 per cent. on the first cost value on board. The unmanufactured leaf is the form of tobacco used by the people, and a duty of from 80 to 140 per cent. on its value seems too much ; manufactured tobacco pays at Barbados, Trinidad, Jamaica, and the Windward Islands about 35 per cent. on its value; at British Guiana 50 per cent., and in the Leeward Islands from about 14 per cent to 20 per cent. The duty on cigars is about 40 per cent. on their value at Jamaica, it sometimes rises to 30 per cent. in other colonies, it is sometimes only 20 per cent. or less. In some of these colonies the people can grow their own tobacco, and the duty on the unmanufactured article will be protective, as an excise would be impracticable. Perhaps the majority of the tariffs were so intended. A lesser, and uniform, duty on common leaf tobacco would probably be more remunerative than the present tariffs.

The duties on articles of ordinary merchandise, yarns, woven fabrics, leather goods, haberdashery, millinery, earthenware, glass and iron ware, are sometimes as high as, and approximate closely to, similar tariffs in those foreign ports where they are imposed expressly for protection purposes There are considerable variations, for apparently no reasons, between the tariffs of the several colonies, which must be very bewildering to merchants and shippers. The Bahama Islands demand 20 per cent., St. Lucia 10 per cent. and 20 per cent., Dominica, St. Vincent, and Grenada 10 per cent., Tobago, Montserrat and Virgin Islands 7½ per cent., Antigua 6 per cent., British Guiana 5 per cent., St. Kitts and Nevis 8 per cent. and 10 per cent., Barbados and Trinidad ask only 4 per cent., which is about the duty that ought to prevail.

Some of the islands have special additions to all customs' duties, for the purpose of meeting special losses from hurricanes, bad crops, or depression in trade ; Dominica makes a surcharge of 20 per cent., Jamaica one of 10 per cent., and Antigua 12½ per cent.

There is no charge on coal entering Jamaica, Trinidad, Bahamas, or St. Lucia, but all the other colonies make a charge ; at St. Vincent it is 10 per cent., Grenada and Virgin Island 7½ per cent., St. Kitts and Nevis 8 per cent. on cost price. Barbados demands 2s. 6d., Antigua 2s. 1d., Dominica 4s. 2d., Montserrat 2s., and British Guiana 1s. 6d. per ton. Salt is allowed to enter Barbados and British Guiana free ; there is a protective tariff at the Bahamas of 20 per cent., and at Turk's Island of 10 per cent. *ad valorem ;* in the other colonies the duty at entry varies between 5 per cent. and 10 per cent. *ad valorem.* The duties on mineral and other oils are unusually heavy, but vary much. St. Christopher and Nevis charge only 8 per cent., Barbados demands 2½d. a gallon or about 35 per cent. on petroleum, and 4 per cent. only on other oils. Jamaica charges 9d. a gallon, the Bahamas and British Guiana 7½d. a gallon (about 100 per cent.), Trinidad charges 6d. a gallon on cocoa-nut oil, and 1s. a gallon on other oils, which will be 150 per cent. on petroleum. The evenings are not long in the tropics, but the duty on this article of universal use by the people should not be so enormous in proportion to its value.

It is to be observed that—except at Barbados, where the duty is 4 per cent., and Grenada, which charges 5 per cent. —machinery, and some metals and metal work, and all articles employed by planters in cultivation and in the manufacture of sugar, rum, and other produce, are free of duty; also all manures. Of course, it is said these exemptions are for the purpose of encouraging planting enterprise. It is good that it should be encouraged, but the poor man pays on everything, whether imported for his trade or not. It is satisfactory to have to note that fresh meat, poultry, turtle, fresh fish, green fruit, and vegetables are usually free of duty.

On the whole, it will be seen that taxation is so adjusted that it falls almost entirely on the labouring population, and the system of tariffs are not only altogether opposed to free trade principles in the abstract, but must act injuriously on the welfare of the population under any theory of taxation.

The West India colonies, with the exception of Barbados, British Guiana, and Honduras, levy export duties. In Jamaica it is 5s. 9d. on a hogshead of sugar, 4s. 6d. on a puncheon of rum, 6s. on a tierce of coffee, and 1s. a ton on dye woods. Trinidad charges 6s. on a hogshead of sugar, and 4s. 4d. on 100 gallons of rum ; molasses, cocoa, coffee, petroleum, and asphalt are also taxed on exportation. Antigua charges 5s. on a hogshead of sugar. St. Christopher and Nevis make export charges on sugar, rum, molasses, arrowroot, cotton, and charcoal. St. Vincent charges sugar, rum, molasses, arrowroot, cotton, and cocoa. Grenada, in addition to the above, adds spices. Dominica and Montserrat tax everything they export. The Bahamas tax guano and cave-earth 2s. a ton, and 1½ per cent. *ad valorem* on everything exported that has not already paid an import duty. The Virgin Islands tax the cattle and provisions they export to the neighbouring port of St. Thomas, and 7½ per cent on wrecked goods.

Export duties are almost universally condemned as a system for providing revenue, even when the exporting countries can claim a monopoly of the article exported. There may be local circumstances, nevertheless, which would make such a form of tax one of the least objectionable in some colonies. Where the only alternatives are duties on imports (places where no other form of tax can be levied) it may be desirable to apply both.

In the West India colonies there are taxes on dogs, horses, cattle, mules, vehicles. It is usual to require licences for many things besides the selling of spirits, tobacco, and stamps; but every colony has a system and tariff of its own on all these matters. Antigua demands 10s. a year for permission to sell bread. Dominica thinks the butcher and blacksmith the right men to pay, and charges them 20s. each. St. Lucia demands 60s. a year from the petroleum dealer, and Grenada 50s. a year from the retailer of charcoal. Boatmen, porters, hawkers, and others are usually licensed by the year by paying certain sums.

There is a poll-tax at St. Lucia, Tobago and Grenada, Dominica, Montserrat, and Virgin Islands, where each male inhabitant up to a certain age is to give so many days' work in each year or pay a stated fine. This is a tax usually in connection with the repair of roads. Roads are of equal use to everybody, and it is of the first necessity that they should be kept up. Some other form of assessment would be fairer to all, and more legitimate. The present tax is unequal; the man who earns 20s. a day pays the same fine as the man who earns 6d. There are taxes on houses and lands, but the latter tax is extremely light. Cane pays 2 dollars an acre in British Guiana, and when empoldered, but not under cane, 2 cents an acre; in the other colonies it varies from 6d. to 1s. 6d. an acre for cane, and 1½d. to 6d. an acre for other land. But in some colonies there is no land-tax of any kind. With respect to houses the taxation varies greatly, but is nowhere heavy.

The Jamaica tax on stock, 1s. a head, seems to act injuriously on the rearing of cattle, for which some parts of the island are suitable, and the import duty of 10s. each on horses and cattle would be better suppressed. There seems no reason why the rearer of cattle should be specially taxed more than the raisers of any other form of produce.

A tax may be bad, but its removal may nevertheless be impracticable all at once. A principle demonstrably right when once departed from cannot always be restored without some straining. If the principles of free trade had been really kept in view by the authorities responsible for the tariffs in Crown colonies, say for the last ten or fifteen years, and if they had really wished to see the system that had been adopted by the people of the United Kingdom adopted also in the colonies under Crown government, as far as circumstances made it practicable, there would be little now left to complain of, because it is certain the present system would have been gradually re-modelled. On the contrary, it is evident that high, and even restrictive, and, therefore, impolitic, tariffs on imports have tended to increase, and the policy of free trade has not been supported in the colonies in places where it easily might have been followed with advantage to themselves and to the trade of the United Kingdom.

In the present condition of these colonies it is easy to put the finger on taxes whose removal would be a vast benefit. It is not so easy to suggest others to replace those removed. But it can be demonstrated that the revenue, as a whole, is unnecessarily large. In every country the revenue must be somewhat in proportion to that amount which the people can afford to pay. If the present taxes are demonstrably too heavy, and are draining the vitality of the people, they should be reduced. The expenses of administration must be made to fit in with the necessities of the position.

Those who advocate protective duties in the United Kingdom, because of their almost universal application on the continent of Europe, overlook the intense misery, low position, inadequate wages, and dangerous discontent of the populations who have to labour and suffer and submit to the tremendous tariffs of France, Italy, Germany, and Russia. It is easy also to point to Canada, to the United States, and to the Australian colonies, where free trade does not exist, for it matters very little at present to the people who inhabit these countries what freaks are played with their enormous natural resources. The absurdity of comparisons of this nature are best shown by figures. Were the United Kingdom to pay Government taxes at the same rate per head as the people of Australasia, the revenue to be raised would be about 240 millions sterling a year. Notwithstanding this taxation—voluntarily imposed and but slightly felt, which would crush the life out of any European state in two or three years—when these Australian governments want to borrow money every one is desirous to lend, and the loans reach a premium which the most powerful monarchies in Europe (so sadly in want of money) could never hope to obtain for their best guaranteed stock. None of the Crown colonies are any way near the pre-eminent position of actual and prospective wealth attained by these rich and really powerful communities ; for, in fact, the people of most Crown colonies are less able to bear burdens than the poorest and most backward nations in Europe. It is curious to note how little accumulated wealth exists in any of these Crown colonies. The trumpery sums paraded in the savings' banks are almost all the accumulated savings possessed by the industrious classes, in the face of comparatively enormous exports extending over years. But the fact is that the trade and wealth of a country must be measured by what it receives and retains as well as by what it gives. If the people had some money over after buying food, almost always heavily taxed, they would spend more in British and other manufactures, in household furniture and other commodities. The larger amount of wages distributed of late years in some of these Crown colonies, among a larger number of labourers for raising a larger quantity of produce, has most of it gone to buy enormously taxed food. There was little surplus over for a larger purchase of British or any other goods.

High duties on imports, in order that all other forms of taxation may be avoided, and the introduction of a low class labour to compete with native labour where such exists, and beat it down to their conditions, may suit planters and absentees and those who look to the raising of produce for export as the end and aim of all colonial policy, but it does not and cannot advantage the colony as a whole, and it is, at the same time, undoubtedly detrimental to the interests of British manufacturers and British working men, the best and most natural markets for whose goods are thereby restricted. A free trade policy would lessen the cost of food and, by leaving a balance over after the primary necessaries of life had been supplied, lead to a larger consumption of, and consequently to a larger demand for, British merchandise. The United Kingdom cannot expect to do a larger or more profitable trade with a pauper community. The tropical Crown colonies will never manufacture certain goods; the better off the people become the more they will take of such goods from the United Kingdom.

The consequences of this fiscal system of high tariffs in the West India colonies has resulted in a demand for what may be called their commercial annexation to the United States. The United States show no unwillingness to annex all the trade and commerce of these colonies, but is adverse to assuming the responsibilities and probable annoyances of a political union. The upshot of the question is that the British Government has been requested to make a treaty with the United States by which their merchandise may enter the West Indies free, but British and other merchandise to continue to be taxed, and for this favour West India produce is to enter United States ports on the same terms as the produce of countries with which similar compacts have been made. The West India colonies have been so badly treated by all parties, and their condition, in consequence, has been often so desperate, that no reasonable man can feel surprised at a demand which under ordinary circumstances and conditions would seem preposterous. It is to be hoped the recent rise in the value of sugar will give breathing-time, and another chance to the responsible authorities to place matters on a sound footing, without it being necessary to have recourse to such desperate means.

It is clear that the remedy in the condition of the West India colonies expected to be brought about by this treaty with the United States would, under any circumstances, be only temporary, and would certainly before very long prove entirely delusive. Reasons for this view are not wanting. The sugar produced within the States themselves is every year increasing in quantity very considerably, and, ultimately, will not only suffice for the wants of the States but there may be a surplus for exportation. The United States have entered already into conventions with most of the sugar-producing countries in Central America, and, before long, they will have concluded similar arrangements with Haïti and San Domingo, and the Spanish West Indies, and others. Under these circumstances British West India sugar will certainly find a worse market at New York than at London, the best market of the world. But meanwhile an irrevocable arrangement will have been made with the United States which will place British goods for ever at a disadvantage in the oldest colonies of the United Kingdom, colonies for which, in days now seemingly forgotten, she fought hard and spent treasure in millions.

A recent United States Consular Report from Jamaica recommends this reciprocity treaty between the United States and the West Indies. The consul was dissatisfied with the course of trade, for although the island took from the United States, in 1883, imports valued at £423,412, only about £10,000 consisted of dry goods and clothing, the remainder being food stuffs; while, during the same year, out of a total of imports amounting to £941,758 from the United Kingdom, £490,000 was the value of dry goods and clothing. A reciprocity treaty would, the consul thinks, reverse the course of trade. It is not quite so certain that it would do so to the complete satisfaction of the consul unless, indeed, the West Indies put a high duty on British imports and permitted free access to United States merchandise. This is, indeed, what was one time aimed at, if not proposed, for the only and declared object of the United States was to shut out United Kingdom dry goods in favour of their own; they would have little or nothing to gain otherwise by the treaty. Had the treaty been concluded on the lines ultimately agreed upon by the United States and supported by the West India committee —the mouthpiece of the absentee interest—the United Kingdom would have been, to a considerable extent, at all events, placed at a disadvantage as regards her general commercial policy, and markets worth some three millions a year for her goods would have been weakened. The West India committee of London is apparently not interested in the production of British manufactures, but their own clients will be the chief sufferers hereafter should the necessities of the position make a treaty necessary, giving the United States a preference over foreign countries and even over Great Britain herself in her own colonies.

There is a danger, not apparently foreseen by those who will mostly suffer from it, in endeavouring to force trade from its natural channels and outlets by conventions such as those proposed between the United States and the West Indies. The

West Indies receive from certain other foreign countries about £1,000,000 a year in the aggregate above the amount they export to these countries direct, and this has to be paid for. The paths of commerce are devious and complicated, and the best and most profitable methods, when nothing interferes, are sure to be found and developed ; at present, the United Kingdom is the large receptacle of produce, and the balances due to other countries are easily paid through her. Even the United States take from the West Indies nearly £500,000 a year less than they send. If the West Indies receive no more British goods, can the London market continue to absorb their produce? Will the course of trade that sets in with the United States be such as to enable the valuable foreign commerce of these colonies, which is not balanced by remittances of produce to them, to be carried on as effectively as it is now? Will the United States be able to absorb the five or six millions sterling of produce now annually shipped to the United Kingdom for home consumption and distribution, if they send no equivalent in return, or only the equivalent the United Kingdom now sends?

No reference to the West India colonies would be satisfactory to the great interests involved without dwelling somewhat on the land laws. It is satisfactory to note the advance of opinion on this question ; these laws have now been unequivocally condemned by every competent authority, and even those most interested in their maintenance are ashamed any longer to stand by them in the face of the universal condemnation. Unfortunately, it is, nevertheless, urgently necessary to keep the question before the public, for every one knows how long an acknowledged abuse may exist in a dependency without any serious efforts being made for its final removal. The consignee's lien may have no longer its acknowledged champions, but there are yet powerful interests not above profiting by the injustice allowed by the law, and these interests will hinder, by methods known to interested partisans, the promised reform. The "consignee's lien," in these days, when the only hope for the West Indies and their inhabitants is in commercial freedom, is particularly iniquitous, unjust, and impolitic; due to it, property has no stability, industry in land has no certain rights, and enterprise and capital have no secure outlet in these colonies. A decision of the High Court of Justice, at Barbados, a year or two back, defeated the attempt to introduce priority for the consignee's lien into that island.

The theory has for a long time been abandoned with respect to the West Indies that they should be ruled and governed for the benefit of an absentee planting interest, but in practice they are nearly as much so now as in any previous period. Politically, the people may have all that can be desired; education, also, has made sound beginnings, and the administration in all its parts and details is honourable and impartial; the ordinary civil and criminal laws are equal for all classes and colours, and they are administered with an impartiality and intelligence found nowhere outside of British rule. Yet the people are poor and degraded because the industries by which they live are weighed down and overborne by special systems which, to say the least, are opposed to every fundamental principle of right and justice known to Englishmen. So certain is it that the economical systems in force in any country are those which have most effect on a people's welfare. When a country is ruled by the most highly educated and intelligent classes, it is a grand thing to see the general welfare alone cared for and ably administered; but it is a sorry and degrading sight to see these privileges misused for personal ends. The inhabitants of the West Indies, by whose efforts alone the absentee merchants can claim to be wealthy, are unjustly over-burdened by a policy by which the interests of the merchants alone profit. In the West Indies, with a few exceptions, the economical systems and mortgage laws are framed entirely in the interests of this class, and so sweepingly and specially, that the natural owners and cultivators of the land have been ousted from it, ruined, and discouraged. This absentee class, through its agents, has by the very use and enjoyment of these special privileges, extending over many years, accumulated enormous power in the various islands, and it can now use this power and influence, and the power and influence its position and wealth gives it at home, to hinder the enactment of those just measures the position of these colonies so urgently need. The "Consignee's Lien," the badge of the commercial servitude of the West Indies, replaced that other servitude of slavery, and therefore the freedom that was given to the inhabitants by the righteousness of the British people was much of it surreptitiously snatched from them by a cunningly devised law, which left them the forms of independence, but took from them the fruits of their toil. How much of the sugar now shipped to London would find other markets if the nominal owners had power to dispose of it can never be known, for London is a good market for every one. No law could be devised by the ingenuity of man which could so effectually hand over the agricultural interests of a whole people to a single monopoly as the " Consignee's Lien."

The late Royal Commission made proposals of a rose-water character, which, if adopted, would only consolidate for a further period the stern evils under which the West India people labour. How can it benefit a poor, ill-fed labourer that food should be made unprocurable by him owing to a 20 per cent. tax on its value instead of being unprocurable at a 35 per cent. tax? Can it benefit him to any extent worth naming if a governor gets £1,000 a year less pay, or a colonial secretary has henceforth to do work some one else is now doing? And these paltry savings are only to result, as was recommended, in a further inroad of coolies for the benefit of absentee planters, and destroy and lower still more completely the value of his labour, and take from him the last chances of providing for his starving children. Are the English people really aware of the condition of the West Indies? Is it not true that among all those islands noted for the value of their exported produce not one could exist without imported food? And how is it there is a growing desire among the people, even of those islands renowned of old for their loyalty, to be severed from the British Empire, and to take refuge and shelter under the flag of the United States, if things are as they should be? Is it not the unendurable ills they are made to bear that forces them? And now that the evil is accomplished, and the ruin can no longer be altogether averted, what is proposed even in England? A convention with the United States. What is this convention to be? Anything that can really benefit the people should be done even at a national loss. Every country in the end, the same as every individual, will have to pay the penalty of injustice and wrong ; and if the people of the United Kingdom lose much or all of the trade of these islands, they will then be able to appreciate the advantages of having abandoned the concerns of a whole people to be dealt with by a selfish monopoly. There is another remedy, not to the evil—for much ruin, misery, starvation, disease, and death will ensue whatever be done—but to ward off further and yet greater evils, perhaps insurrection and bloodshed, for it must not be expected the people will starve quietly—and that

c

remedy is to sweep away unconditionally all these food duties, and to reduce the cost of administration. A fewer number of high judicial and other officials, and a lesser number of governors, should suffice in these days of steam and telegraphs.

It is almost unnecessary to advocate any further the rights of the labouring population of these dependencies of the Crown to have their labour utilised in the cultivation of the land they have to live in. The importation of coolies has recently developed pressing dangers which will tend more to put a stop to the traffic than the plainest statements of rights and duties. It is almost certain that those colonies which have already more than enough people for all the labour that can possibly be wanted in them will not be flooded with contracted for pauper coolie labour from India, on the untrue ground that the native-born labourer is idle, incompetent, and unreliable. If men are really free, they have a right to have some voice in the question of their wages. The importation of foreign workmen into England when the building trades were on strike was not popular with people of any class ; not even with those who deemed that the workmen were wrong in their demands.

The population of the West India colonies, at the close of 1883, was about 1,537,250. In the coolie colonies of Trinidad and British Guiana, the males outnumbered the females by 22 per cent., in the remaining colonies the females exceeded the males by 18 per cent. Taking all the colonies, each inhabitant paid 13s. 7d. customs duties, chiefly on food stuffs, in 1883. The labouring classes pay as much of these taxes as any one else, if not more. A man and wife and three children would pay 67s. 11d. in customs charges in the year, even on the insufficient diet they could procure. If a family do not eat the flour and other food actually taxed, but only the roots procurable in the market, they pay the taxes nevertheless, because the prices of these articles accommodate themselves to the prices of the flour and other taxed foods and rice, there not being over a tenth enough of such root crops for the people's consumption anywhere, sometimes not one-twentieth.

Wages will be as follows, on an average, for an able-bodied man :—200 days at 20 cents. (10d.), 50 days at 28 cents. (1s. 2d.), 50 days at 32 cents. (1s. 4d.), total for 300 days in the year, £14 11s. 8d. Let it be assumed the man has a wife and three children ; the woman, by the custom of the country, will work at field labour, and will earn a third as much as the man, or £4 17s. 2½d ; the three children, on an average, and before they work on their own account. will earn half as much as the woman, or £2 8s. 7d. Total for the family £21 17s. 5½d. in the year. This would be a strictly fortunate and hard-working family ; it assumes no one will be sick, or incapable of work, and that they will all be able to find remunerative work for 300 days in the year. Taking the whole of the West India colonies, the taxation per head in 1883 was a little over £1 6s. 6d. For the family of five this will be £6 12s. 6d., or over 30 per cent. of their total possible earnings ; in Great Britain the proportion is 11·88 (but if the average earnings of agricultural labourers only were considered, it would, perhaps, be more) ; in the United States it is 9·21 ; in Brazil and South America it is 19·25 ; in all Europe it is 15·3 per cent. The family, after paying these taxes, will have £15 4s. 11½d. to live on for the year. The following details are founded on the latest information from reliable sources. Provisions may be purchased at the prices quoted below in the largest ports, where they are cheapest :—Sweet potatoes, 60 to 100 lb. for 4s. 2d. ; yams, 50 to 60 lb. for 4s. 2d. ; eddoes, 40 lb. for 4s. 2d. ; rice (inferior quality), 3 pints for 5d. ; corn meal 2½ lb. for 5d. ; wheaten flour (low grade), 2 lb. for 5d. ; butter, 1 lb. for 2s. ; salt pork and beef, 1 lb. for 9d. ; mutton (very rare), 1 lb. for 1s. ; beef (poor quality), 1 lb., 6d. ; fish, 1 lb., 3d. to 6d. Food has been scarce recently, and is likely to become more so ; the above prices will be much increased (30 to 50 per cent.) in country districts and minor ports, and in some places all of the above provisions will not be obtainable at any price. This industrious and comparatively well-to-do family of five, after paying taxes, will have 10d. per day to live on. Deductions will have to be made for clothing, 5s. per head a year, 25s. ; house (and taxes for same, not included in Government taxes), 30s. per year ; 5s. a year for cooking materials, furniture, and fuel. This will leave about 8d. a day for food for the five persons. Let them buy and eat the lowest-priced articles procurable, and they must pass a life of semi-starvation, and without common decencies, and this for people who have to work hard every working day in the year, and are all able to do so.

C 2

CHAPTER II.

CEYLON.

CEYLON has historically an important and picturesque past. Its present position is one of interest, but it has lost much of its picturesque element. For reasons whose validness, if at any time demonstrable, have never been made evident, the island has been subjected to a fiscal and economical policy which has not led to that prosperity which should ever distinguish British rule. It would not be difficult to prove how a different fiscal and economical policy would have led to more satisfactory results, and have brought more happiness and more prosperity to the old races who inhabit the island. The position is such that it is doubted whether 1,500 years ago the island was not better off than it is now after some centuries of European dominion, of which about ninety years have been British. It is satisfactory, however, to know that, notwithstanding the policy so long 'followed in the island and which is so opposed to everything that is deemed essential to prosperity by all parties in Great Britain, the colony can yet compare advantageously with the adjacent colonies of other nations. Such complimentary comparisions are often made, and, in consequence, it is to be feared that too low a standard is apt to be accepted by legislators and by governors for their platform. A British Crown colony should compare with no other place ; it should stand alone as an example of a sound, enlightened, and generous policy practically exemplified.

When the forced labour—which probably built the tanks, and certainly kept them in repair—and the milder forms of slavery that existed in the island were abolished at the close of the year 1844, no other methods were adopted to keep up the tanks and supply the necessary irrigation for cultivators. Vast districts fell out of cultivation, and had to be abandoned by the population. It is true that before emancipation many of the irrigation works were neglected by the administration, and fell into decay. Some people doubted the wisdom of the abolition of forced labour on account of these results, but it is manifest that this just and statesmanlike act—which was imposed on the local administration by public opinion at home—should have been followed up by the necessary measures to keep established public works in repair. Any form of forced labour is well known to be at least as expensive to the community as paid labour, and, in fact, it is generally more expensive under modern conditions of society and law, and always unjust and irksome. The measure of emancipation was not in entire accordance with the views of the Government officials in the island, and these gentlemen, and their successors, have often pointed out how unwise were the British public to interfere with the gentle, paternal despotism that operated in their Eastern dominions. Forced labour, redeemable by fine, was kept on for the making and repairing of roads, because powerful interests were brought to bear. But the policy of this forced labour is also essentially bad and unwise. In recent times the fatal system of neglecting the tanks has been reversed, and large numbers have been repaired and put to work at considerable cost; between 1869–73, 3,000,000 rupees are stated to have been spent on them, the people finding the money; but a great deal yet remains to be done before the effects of past neglect can be obliterated. The abandonment of the tanks by the British Administration not only ruined thousands of proprietors and families, and caused large cultivated districts to relapse into jungle, but actually cut off the water supply for the consumption of the people, who were forced, in consequence, to drink from polluted sources, and died in vast numbers of the diseases thereby caused.

Forced labour has been recently revived, in some parts, for tank-repairing and the establishment and maintenance of irrigation works; owners of paddy land and villagers being compelled to give a certain number of days labour in each year, in proportion to their holding or interest, or pay a commutation fee. The system has kept tanks in repair, and has resulted in important local irrigation works, that were much needed, being carried through. The Government evidently also gets considerable advantages from these works, in the increase of its revenue from the taxes on grain; it, in fact, reaps the advantage of the tenants' improvements, albeit they have been obtained by compulsory labour. Besides the tanks, there are the necessary methods for the distribution of the water to be made and maintained, and it seems certain obsolete customs have been revived by local ordinances which practically result in a system of forced labour; the villagers being compelled to labour in the irrigation works for a number of days each year, sometimes receiving the average wages of the time and place, sometimes cultivators work without remuneration. Although the village communities (elected by universal suffrage) have been entrusted with some jurisdiction in these matters, it is almost certain the most powerful and influential among the villagers will find means to act unfairly to, if not to oppress, the poorer labourers. Such despotic systems of coercive labour always work that way, wherever they are in operation and however well they may be supervised. It seems the Government charges no water rates when the earth-works have been constructed by the enforced, unpaid, labour of the village cultivators, and it then also supplies, at its own cost (from the public taxes), the necessary masonry and iron-work connected with such works.

It is to be remarked, in connection with this subject, that the making of, and the repairs to, these village tanks and the attendant irrigation works, have vastly benefited the occupiers of the neighbouring lands, and the Government has reaped a large and more certain revenue. On the other hand, in those parts where such systems have not yet been enforced (or rather where village irrigation work has not yet been taken in hand), the land is often in a bad condition, and the revenue, of course, suffers in proportion ; the paddy crops being un-certain, or there being none.

The argument that has naturally followed is that the system of enforced labour is suited to the island, and should be pursued and kept up, at all events for beneficial schemes of recognised public utility. Now an argument of this nature would be valid in any country on similar grounds. It is said the people are paid in those cases where it is proper they should be. But why should paid labour be forced unless the remuneration be inadequate? Why are not the railways also constructed by the forced labour of those who want them and who benefit by them, if it be the system suitable to the island, and for the construction of important works? What are wanted in Ceylon, as in all tropical colonies, are good communications and serviceable irrigation works, and as these cannot be made at Ceylon, more than anywhere else, without costing their full value in labour and in material to some one, why not have them constructed, even as other public works are, by con-tract, and payable, as other public works are, by taxation or by loan? Why pursue a method degrading to the people, and certain to impede, for years to come, any of that real advance which depends more on an independent self-reliance, and a consciousness of freedom of action and absence of restraint than on anything else? This revival and copying of Oriental despotic systems, even though they should be always applied with benevolent intelligence, is unworthy of a British administration, and is decidedly unsafe, however well it may be guided, and however ably it may be conducted; and, in fact, by such actions the local administrations are opposing the determination arrived at by the Parliament and Government of the United Kingdom nearly fifty years ago. The whole island paid for the railways that opened the hill country to British planters and capitalists, but the work required for irrigation purposes by the people themselves in their villages must be accomplished, it appears, by the unwilling, because enforced, labour of the local inhabitants, and be paid for on different principles. The Government profits more largely from these works than from any others. Much has been said about the advantages of these village communities, by which the country people are permitted to manage some of their own concerns, but in this respect they are only taxing machines. The administration itself must not employ forced labour or similar methods repugnant to the people of the United Kingdom, but it appears to think it may depute the power of doing so to others. Local bodies with real power may be much wanted in all the Crown colonies, but certainly not local bodies with mediæval powers of coercion only.

It is the opinion of many high authorities that these irrigation works, undertaken and carried through by the village councils, which the administration sets to work, guides, and instructs, have been of great use. It is a misfortune that it should have been deemed requisite to have had recourse to such methods. It is impossible to justify enforced labour, especially in countries where it is so necessary to plant other notions among the people, and the use of such labour makes less favourable the contrast of British rule and authority with the despotic and unjust, as well as impolitic, systems known to be employed in Java, Sumatra, and other neighbouring places. It makes it really impossible for Englishmen to denounce oppression anywhere.

The opinion is not universally held that the cultivation of paddy is a paying concern in Ceylon, and many good judges hold that it would be better to raise other crops and get the whole of the rice from Burmah or India, where it can be grown much cheaper. Irrigation by tanks is useful and necessary for many other kinds of produce besides rice. The natural irrigation by river overflow in the great rice countries not only conveys moisture but manure. Sir C. P. Layard (a great Ceylon authority) deems rice cultivation in Ceylon the least profitable of pursuits for a native. To unprejudiced lookers-on it will appear as if the administration would not have interested itself so much in the matter were it not for the revenues derivable from grain. Irrigation will be wanted whatever may be the cultivation of the future. It is to be hoped a man's ordinary freedom of action will be allowed him in Ceylon, even should he reside where a village council holds sway.

The Government railways have been made from Colombo to the coffee and mountain districts; the money was raised by debenture loans, repayable by sinking funds. This is an outlay that was primarily almost entirely made in the interest of planters, but it will be of use to the island, although not of such immediate and permanent value as the restoration of the tanks and the spread of irrigation works on which the main agricultural interest of the people must always depend. In course of time railways will probably be extended over the whole island, and not into coffee and planting districts only. There were 178 miles of railway completed, and more under construction, at the close of 1883. There were also about 1,100 miles of telegraph-wires in use. As in all mountainous countries, subjected to a heavy and fitful rainfall, roads are difficult to be kept in effective repair, and this is no doubt one of the causes of that other special forced labour or road tax being continued. It will also be a reason why railways, in such countries, are generally a practical and economical necessity, and pay for their construction fairly well, nearly as well as the tanks.

The population in 1881 was about 2,764,000, the males being in excess by about 180,000; the 160,000 to 200,000 Tamils (Malabars or coolies), who come over from the coast of Coromandel and Southern India every year for several weeks or months to labour for the estates and on the public works, have comparatively few women among them, the more resident coolie labourers the same. The island races are divided into Cingalese, who number about three-fifths of the whole population, Tamils (Malabars) one-fifth, and Moors (Indo Arabs) nearly one-fifth. The remaining races, mixed and pure, comprise together only about 1 per cent. of the whole, and include the Europeans, the Burghers and Eurasians (descendants of Portuguese and Dutch settlers and mixed races) Veddahs, Parsees, Javanese, Afghans, and others.

In Ceylon the Government is the landlord. There are about 2,600,000 acres of land under different forms and degrees of cultivation. The amount of land privately held has been variously estimated; there is the Government estimate and there are other estimates from private sources which conflict. Some of the total estimated acreage of the island (15,909,000 acres) will be unavailable and unremunerative for cultivation purposes; deduction will also have to be made for foreshore, water, roads, and railways, but all of these are rendered remunerative for fiscal purposes by the revenue officials; further large deductions will have to be made from the possible cultivated area for forest reserves and other purposes not necessarily unremunerative to the administration. It is evident there is room for a large increase of the various industries connected with land. Of the cultivated land, some is privately held, having been purchased, but some is held on terms of yearly payment to the administration. The land held by planters has been sold to them; land has also been reputedly sold to native cultivators, but the sale is often an apparent one only, for almost all cultivators of grain and paddy have to pay a tithe of their produce, yearly, which practically amounts to a rent charge, from which raisers of other forms of produce are exempted. It has been shown that paddy cultivators are also compelled to make and keep up village tanks and irrigation systems. The land at present unalienated may be said to belong to the Government of Ceylon, in trust for the people of the island; much of it, indeed, consists of jungle and waste occupied and cultivated by the inhabitants in times more or less remote, before cultivation, villages, communities, and towns depreciated and fell away, and the misfortunes that ever attend on war and conquest overtook the Cingalese. The forest lands are said to amount to $2\frac{3}{4}$ millions of acres.

The 2,600,000 acres in cultivation (including natural pasturage) in the year 1883-4 comprised about 736,000 acres for different grain and rice, 293,000 acres for coffee, 950,000 acres for palms and natural pasturage, 260,000 acres for cocoanuts, 36,000 acres for cinnamon, 40,000 acres for cinchona, about 20,000 acres for tea plants, and 42,000 acres for cotton; 38,000 acres for cardamoms, vanilla, cacao, ginger, spices, and cultivated grass; 185,000 acres for different kinds of fruit and cane (the people make a considerable quantity of jaggery sugar for their own use from certain of their palm trees, and obtain sago from others). It is to be observed that these estimates are open to some variation in detail. A large capital is invested in the higher class of cultivation, commonly called the "planting industry," and more is being continually added. Certain products, such as coffee, sometimes fall off, and others, such as tea, have more ground given to them; but the above figures will give a fair idea of the position for the year 1883-4.

The chief produce raised for exportation is plantation coffee. In 1884 the amount was 13½ millions rupees, of which Great Britain took about £1,082,000. [In 1880 the value of this article exported came to £3,124,000—a small proportion is native grown. In 1881 the value was £2,000,000, and £1,685,000 in 1882.] In the same year, 1884, cinchona, valued at about 4¼ millions rupees was raised, and nearly 1½ millions rupees in tea. Cacao (a recent introduction) gave 323,000 rupees. The cinnamon cultivation is almost entirely in the hands of the natives, the average yearly export for ten years (1874-83) was nearly £75,000. The areca palm nut is largely consumed in the island; there was an average export of about £93,000 annually during the ten years 1874-83. The produce of the cocoa-nut tree is chiefly exported in the form of oil, and the amount varies considerably every year; for ten years (1874-83) it averaged nearly £248,000 a year, and the local consumption of nuts and oil will be equal to many times the export. The fibre of the cocoa-nut is utilised in various ways. Plumbago is an important item of export on which the Government charges a royalty of 5½d. per cwt. The average yearly export for seven years (1874-80) was £123,000, and for the three years 1881-83 £244,000; the quantity exported in the ten years was 1,710,000 cwt., bringing £39,187 duty. The total produce of the island exported in 1884 is estimated to have been less in value than that of the previous year by 1,882,889 rupees. Ceylon re-exports some imports, but this trade also fell off in 1884 from previous years; it fell off nearly 950,000 rupees in 1884, compared with 1883.

The imports of bullion and specie into Ceylon for the fifteen years 1869–83 amounted to about £11,600,000, largely from India, of which only about £1,341,000 appears as being re-exported. Some of this large balance probably remained in the island (the savings banks have about £200,000), but the greater part certainly has not remained, and much of it was doubtless taken home by the returning Tamil labourers and others leaving the island, and would not figure in any returns.

The total imports into Ceylon for the fifteen years 1869–83 were about 75¼ millions sterling, and the total exports 64 millions, a difference of 11¼ millions; but 10½ millions of this is accounted for in the specie returns above. For the two years 1882–83 the total imports were about £8,900,000, and the total exports £6,740,000. In 1884 the imports were 51,322,142 rupees (£4,811,450), of which 7,837,792 rupees (£734,793) was specie, and the exports were 33,720,134 rupees (£3,161,262), of which only 211,845 rupees (£19,860) was specie. In 1883 the imports of specie were 5,190,669 rupees (£486,625).

In the 8 years, 1869–76, the imports from Australasia amounted to £1,506,000, and the exports to Australasia to £406,000. In the 7 years, 1877–83, the imports from Australasia were only £313,000, and the exports thereto were £504,000; during the first period Australasia sent £1,100,000 more than she received, and in the latter period she received £90,000 more than she sent, with a diminished trade. On the other hand, in the 12 years ending 1883, the United States received £1,983,000, but there are only about £4,000 imports from that country during this period. In the 10 years 1874–83, Austria took nearly £3,000,000, but exported to Ceylon very little in return; in the 5 years 1879–83, the proportions were 18 to 1. During the 10 years ending 1883, France and her possessions sent £2,400,000, and took £1,700,000 in return. There was a balance due to them (£700,000) which was probably paid in bills. There was but a slight trade with Hong Kong, Mauritius, and Suez, and about £30,000 to £40,000 a year imports from the Maldive Islands.

The trade with the United Kingdom shows exports amounting to £28,821,000 for the 10 years, 1866–75; an average of £2,882,000 a year, and £17,331,000 for the 5 years, 1875–80; an average of £3,466,000. The value of imports from the United Kingdom (including bullion and specie, when given, and foreign and colonial produce and manufactures) for the 10 years, 1866–75, was about £14,070,000, an average of £1,407,000 a year; for the 5 years, 1876–80, it was £7,167,000, an average of £1,433,000 a year. During the 15 years, 1866–80, Ceylon sent to the United Kingdom £46,152,000, and took £21,237,000 (including specie).

In the 3 years, 1881–83, the exports to the United Kingdom amounted to £5,924,000 (Ceylon valuation), an average of £1,974,000 a year; and the imports from the United Kingdom were £3,676,000, an average of £1,225,000 a year (including bullion, specie, and foreign and colonial produce shipped from Great Britain).

The imports of manufactured cotton and twist averaged £855,200 a year for the 10 years, 1867–76, and £572,400 for the 5 following years, 1877–81. For the 3 years, 1882–84, the average was £490,000 (at 1s. 10½d. a rupee) of which about £247,000 a year was in cotton yarn and piece goods from the United Kingdom. The imports of haberdashery and millinery for the 10 years above mentioned averaged £73,300 a year, and for the 5 years following £89,000 a year, and for 1882–83 £73,000 a year (of which under £19,000 a year was from the United Kingdom). The imports of coal and coke averaged £172,000 a year for the 10 years, 1867–76, and £187,000 for the 5 years, 1877–81. In the 3 years, 1882–84, 556,645 tons were imported (in 1883, the United Kingdom sent 55 per cent.). The imports of cutlery and hardware from all countries averaged £36,000 a year for the 18 years ending 1883, but has been declining of late.

Ceylon, during the 18 years ending 1883, has imported from the United Kingdom £24,913,000, nearly 110 per cent. less in value than she sent to it (£52,056,000). During the same period of 18 years her total imports (including bullion and specie) amounted in value to about 89 millions sterling, and her total exports to about 74¾ millions. The United Kingdom, therefore, sent something over 27½ per cent. of total imports and took about 69½ per cent. of total exports, during that period.

The Board of Trade returns, for the whole 18 years, show the exports to Ceylon from the United Kingdom to be about £7,750,000 (or 45⅙ per cent.) less than the colonial valuations, and the imports from Ceylon to be about £10,000,000 (or 19¼ per cent.) more than the colonial valuations for the same period.

In the year 1882-3 Ceylon imported from India rough and clean rice, grain, wheat, pulse and seeds, weighing 3,278,330 cwt., and in 1883-4 she imported 3,241,190 cwt. In the former year she also imported from India 2,729,034 lb. flour, and 2,938,296 lb. in the latter year. In the 2 years she took from India 8,120,737 lb. salt fish. The imports from India for the 18 years 1866–83 were valued at 55½ millions sterling, being 62 per cent. of total imports. The exports to India for the same period were valued at Ceylon at less than 12 millions sterling.

Next to rice and grains, the most important imports from India consist of cotton goods. In the 9 years ending 1884 their export value was estimated in India at £1,326,251, an average of £147,361 a year. India also sends over £8,000 a year in gunny-bags to pack produce for export. An item of import into Ceylon one would not expect to find is about £17,000 a year from India in vegetables and fruit, fresh fruit and fresh vegetables (some of which are re-exported). Ceylon takes nearly £25,000 a year in sugar from India, and £20,000 a year in special woods.

In the 3 years 1881–3 the duties of customs paid in Ceylon on grain, dried fish, curry stuffs, and sugar alone, all articles chiefly imported from India, were £769,413 (at 1s. 10½d. the rupee).

The total value of grain and paddy imported into Ceylon in the 17 years 1867–83 was over £2,300,000, and of cleaned rice nearly 29½ millions sterling; during the same period the imported salt and dried fish was valued at over 1½ million, and curry stuffs were valued at about £880,000. Live stock, cattle, &c., were valued at £1,085,000, and poonac (to feed cattle and poultry and for other purposes) at £1,020,000. Most of these imports were from India and Burmah, and amounted to £36,285,000. In the 3 years 1882-4, the value of the above articles imported, amounted to 44 per cent. of the total imports of the colony. The quantity of rice alone was 16,764,400 bushels, valued at £5,110,000, being 37¼ per cent. of total imports during those years. The import duties levied on this rice at 29 cents a bushel was £455,782 (at 1s. 10½d. the rupee), about 9 per cent. on its declared value. During the same 3 years paddy and other grain was imported into Ceylon, the duty on which at 29 cents a bushel for grain, and 13 cents a bushel on paddy, came to about £45,000.

In the same period the tax levied on grain grown in the island itself was about £276,000. This makes a total grain tax of £776,782 in 3 years, or the same proportion as if the United Kingdom paid about £3,400,000 each year on corn imported and grown at home. For a rich country like England this would be thought serious, but Ceylon is a poor country, where the wages of common manual labour are only a fraction of the like wages in England, and the tax is levied almost entirely on rice, the food of the poor. But these are not the only charges; home-grown grain has further burdens to bear. The Government tax (or rent) on lands under grain or paddy cultivation varies; it is sometimes more than one-tenth on paddy lands, but the tenants may redeem the annual extra charge, when more than the tenth, by effecting a commutation of it on the basis of a twenty years' assessment, and paying this amount in four instalments. From lands under fine grain, and not adapted for paddy cultivation, a tenth of the yearly produce only is exacted; Kandyan territories are exempted. The excise tax on grain has this much to be said in its favour, that it causes the Administration to be directly interested in the production of rice and grain, and consequently in the maintenance and spread of irrigation works. But the Administration could perform this essential duty for the people and obtain the necessary revenue more equitably. It is for statesmen and administrators to devise the best methods, and to abolish those which are bad. The taxes have no doubt fallen on uncomplaining shoulders. In fact, the cultivators of grain and paddy may not themselves object to the tax; it raises the cost of an article they produce, but which it should be the interest of every one else to make cheaper. No sound reasons can be advanced for continuing to impose a tax of this nature on a special industry when so many other sources from which revenue could be obtained are comparatively untouched. It is as well, also, to candidly acknowledge that taxes of this class-character lower the prestige of British administration; it is so evident that the same standard is not applied to the people who have a voice in these matters, and those who are administered patriarchially by an intelligent and benevolent despotism.

The Administration is composed of a Governor, an

Executive Council of five officials, and a Legislative Council of nine officials and six non-officials, the latter being all nominees of the Governor.

If all cultivated lands were to be taxed alike, instead of those only under a particular produce raised exclusively by natives, and the most useful and essential one of all, and the least remunerative to cultivate, the Administration would come in contact with classes of cultivators of a very different type from the docile and submissive Cingalese. But no British Administration need fear doing right. A tax when spread over a larger area could be much lower in proportion for all. There is a point also of some moment to be thought of in these questions, and that is, who consumes, or would consume if they could, the most British merchandise, the absentee planter or the people? After nearly a century of British rule, Ceylon takes yearly less of British produce and manufactures; the people are too poor to pay for more. The great prosperity so often talked of was simply the raising of produce for export, which planters sent to London because it happened to be the best market for its sale, and will probably continue to be so more and more. If the industrial and economical history of the Crown colonies proves anything, it is that this form of progress, when forced beyond its natural growth, is not of much permanent use to a colony or to its inhabitants, and it confers but little benefit on British industries. Except the planters, who are mostly absentees, the only people who profit at all are the merchants who deal in the produce, and the carriers of it. The money spent in wages gets distributed no doubt among the people, but these wages are terribly low, and it is seen the people have to spend most of them in buying Indian rice and paying the heavy taxes levied on it, and on their home-grown grain. Mr. John Fergusson, a most distinguished authority, in his work, "Ceylon in 1883," says:—
"We have no reserve fund of past profits to fall back upon. . . . Money has been sent here to fell our forests and plant them with coffee, and it has been returned in the shape of copious harvests to the home capitalist, leaving us in some cases the bare hill-sides from whence these rich harvests were drawn." The speculation was undoubtedly a good one; Mr. Fergusson calculates (in 1883) that 18,000,000 cwt. of coffee were raised on 320,000 acres of plantations since 1849, the cost was 42s. per cwt., and it sold at 60s. per cwt., a profit of

£17,000,000 in the aggregate. He laments lands now lying waste that for years enriched the owners. He might have added, the absentee owners who paid no taxes.

As Mr. R. Giffen stated at the Statistical Society's meeting, on the 21st February, 1882, "It is quite conceivable that a country may be very prosperous without foreign trade at all, or with very little foreign trade, or that for special reasons the foreign trade of the least prosperous country, as a whole, may be making greater progress than the foreign trade of a more progressing country. The progress of the foreign trade of different countries is thus no index at all as to their relative progress materially." Another important authority, Mr. Bourne, said : "Russia exports £50,000,000 of corn a year, but her people are worse fed, housed, and clothed than perhaps any other nation in Europe." The conclusion that must be arrived at is, that the raising of produce for export is a considerable factor in the progress of a colony, if the people inhabiting the colony are those who profit by the industry; but it is not necessarily the most important one when they do not do so ; and no administration will be doing its duty if it confers on an absentee planters' industry special facilities at the expense of the general population.

It is not easy to describe the system so as to bring it home to Englishmen, and make it understood by them, this system of looking at a colony chiefly as a produce exporter; it has been so often praised, and taken as a standard of the highest administrative ability. But supposing at their own Norman conquest the conquerors, instead of becoming Englishmen, had remained strangers, and had likewise brought over foreign serfs for a term of years from the Continent to cultivate the land, but not permanently to dwell on it, and had paid these serfs out of the proceeds of cultivation just enough for them to live on while they remained, and then exported the whole of the crops so raised to the Continent, and pocketed the value, the English people (the Saxon serfs) having nothing to do in the matter, and having no concern in the industry that was exhausting the best selected soil of their country. They must also imagine the Saxon serfs had to get the food they could not raise on the plots of land they were allowed to occupy from abroad, and pay high duties on its entry, paying a like duty on the grain they raised for themselves. It is said, of course, the people in the colonies prefer this system, because they will not work themselves, and, in fact, do not wish to do so. The Tamils in Ceylon, and the coolies in the West Indies, may be thought by some to be as the Irish coming across to assist in the English harvest, but the conditions are not by any means the same. The results of the system speak for it, and prove it to be one by which no country can permanently advance in wealth, and no home of a people can ever be made happy and prosperous. The cultivation of a country is never on a secure basis except it be in the hands of the permanent inhabitants, and indissolubly bound up with their family life, their interests, and their hopes. It must not depend only, or even chiefly, for its support and its existence on foreign capital and foreign enterprise. This foreign capital and this enterprise may fail, or they may seek other lands, or, having made the profits sought after, they may retire on the fruits. But a people cannot retire from business; with them the struggle must be eternal and ever to be renewed; the richest and the poorest, the oldest and the newest countries have to struggle and to work; the moment they cease to do this they die.

It is to be remarked that the duty on rice in the husk is 13 cents, and on cleaned rice it is 29 cents a bushel; as it takes rather over 2 bushels of rice in the husk to make 1 bushel of clean rice, this makes the duty on rice in the husk about the same. The export duty from India is the same on rice in the husk as on clean rice (3 annas a maund, about 6⅛d. per cwt.), the consequence is that the importation of rice in the husk into Ceylon is very limited indeed, because, on the whole, it thus pays a higher duty (including Indian and Ceylon duties) than clean rice. In tropical countries rice in the husk will keep a long while, and may be stored up; but cleaned rice is perishable, and rapidly deteriorates. It is obvious that the system pursued, even were duties on grain an unobjectionable form of taxation, is the worst possible; it makes it difficult for the people to take due advantage of a cheap and abundant harvest and low prices to store up grain, and constrains them to live, as it were, from hand to mouth on a perishable and deteriorating commodity. It is well known that people often prefer to purchase the article that is ready for immediate use, even if the quality be somewhat inferior to that which might be had by more trouble; but on the score of cheapness and health, it must often be better could the people obtain sound rice in the husk, which they can clean themselves by manual labour, to

D

rice cleaned in India and full of dust and weevils.   In order to
equalise the price of rice in the husk and clean rice to the
people of Ceylon, the former, at all events, should enter the
island free.   It takes much labour to unhusk a bushel of rice.

The salt-tax is not much felt by the bulk of the population,
but it is said to act injuriously on the health of the people who
inhabit remote places ; it undoubtedly hinders agricultural
improvement in well-known directions.

The revenue for the seven years, 1867–73 (at 2s. the
rupee), was £7,464,831 ; for the seven years, 1874–80, it was
£9,792,138 ; for the three years, 1881–83, it was £3,585,434
(at 1s. 10½d. the rupee).   For the first seven years the duties
of customs amounted to 25 per cent. of the revenue, for
the subsequent seven years they amounted to over 20 per cent.
of it, and for the three years, 1881–83, they were about 22 per
cent. of it.   Besides the ordinary revenues, there are local
revenues for local purposes, amounting to about £200,000 a
year.   Municipal bodies are elected in Ceylon by a high and
therefore limited franchise.

There is an item of revenue which exists in this colony
(and, indeed, in too many other of the Crown colonies) which
compels every male between the ages of 18 and 55 to give six
days' work a year on the roads, or pay 1 rupee 50 cents
(2 rupees in Colombo).   If, as with a conscription, every
man physically capable were compelled to work the six days,
the law would be absurd, but it would be just in the
abstract.   At present it amounts to an unjust tax ; the revenue
from it in 1883 was 704,294 rupees, in 1878 it came to
928,793 rupees.   [Indian coolies employed as agricultural
labourers are exempted, also those seeking employment as
such ; this is an exemption entirely in favour of the planters,
who are the only employers of this foreign labour.]   This
Ceylon law is generally regarded as a remnant of the "Raja-
caria," the forced labour of bygone days.   But the fact is that
colonial officials, when they proceed from one colony to
another, are apt to take with them their old established views
with regard to systems they find operating in some backward
settlement they have been administering, and many colonies
thus get inoculated with views that have been condemned by
every politician and statesman in Europe.   This tax of
1½ rupee is paid equally by the labourer, who only uses the
road by walking on it barefooted as a passenger, and the pro-

prietor who uses it to have brought to his door in waggons and carts every commodity of a well-to-do household. [Of course he pays also for his waggons and carts.] The local price of good able-bodied labour averages 35 cents of a rupee a day, but it is doubtful whether a man between 45 and 55 years of age could earn more than two-thirds of this amount; the $1\frac{1}{2}$ rupee represents $4\frac{1}{2}$ days' work to the average good labourer, and to the middle class man an hour's work. The revenue for general purposes of government amounts to about 8s. $6\frac{1}{4}$d. per head of population; compared with Mauritius this is very low, not quite $4\frac{1}{2}$ rupees per head (the rupee at 1s. $10\frac{1}{2}$d.), against $24\frac{1}{4}$ rupees at Mauritius. But it represents over 13 days' labour to every able-bodied working man in Ceylon (at 35 cents a day), and the same for his wife and each child (because the average of taxation is based on the entire population); together with road labour, and after allowing for certain deductions for family earnings, the taxes the Cingalee adult has to pay represent two months' labour of 26 days each to the working man a year (who has a wife and three children), at the Ceylon rate of wages—35 cents a day = 9 rupees 10 cents a month of 26 days; this at 1s. $10\frac{1}{2}$d. a rupee = 17s. $0\frac{3}{4}$d. For a family of five = $1\frac{17}{8}$d. per day each (30 days to one month).

There is no objection to the amount paid in taxation in Ceylon, if it be raised by safe and sound methods, and wisely expended. Wages, it is seen, are very low, and there is no reason why they should not continue to be so. But in order to increase the quantity and efficiency of this cheap labour it will be necessary to make the food of the people abundant and low-priced. Ricardo laid it down that the natural price of labour was regulated by the cost of food. Exceptions have been taken to this statement; perhaps it should include all other primary wants as well as food. It will always, however, be largely true as regards unskilled labour everywhere.* Sir E. Watkin, M.P., in a letter to the Select Committee of the House of Commons on Irish Industries, dated 25th June, 1885, said :—" When the labourer passes from the stage of underfeeding to that of good nutrition he can do more work, and he always does it." The fiscal systems actually in operation in Ceylon, with regard to food, make it difficult, if not impossible, for the labourer, at

---

* But the *natural* price of labour does not and could not possibly exist in any country where the inhabitants have to compete with coolie or any other form of servile labour, as a part of the social system.

D 2

present wages, to subsist adequately.   There is an excise duty
of at least a tenth on the production of most grain raised in
the island itself.   This is an old form of taxation which may
not have been specially injurious in the olden time when the
people lived and worked under entirely different conditions to
those of the present day.   In those days, also, the tanks and
irrigation works brought richness to every field; there were no
other ways for raising revenue, and commerce, agriculture, and
industry were carried on by different, and defunct, methods,
and the island produced more than was wanted for a population, at the lowest estimate, five times more numerous than
that of the present day.   But Ceylon does not and cannot now
raise enough grain for half its people.   It therefore seeks rice
in India and Burmah.   There is a tax levied on the export of
this article from India at the rate of $6\frac{1}{8}$d. the bushel; it is
taxed again on entering Ceylon at $6\frac{1}{2}$d. the bushel.   It is well
known that many people in the island are driven to find
unwholesome substitutes for the food thus partly placed out of
their reach by fiscal arrangements.

The Government expects to be recouped for the expendi-
ture on irrigation works, irrespective of the tax of $\frac{1}{10}$th and
upwards charged on most corn and grain grown in the island.
A local Ordinance, passed in 1873, enables cultivators to con-
vert the repayment by 10 annual instalments [for the outlay on
works on irrigated lands], into a fixed charge in perpetuity of
one rupee an acre.   When land is not irrigated there is often a
limited crop, and sometimes no crop at all.   The Administration gains by the certainty of abundant harvests and the
attendant prosperity.   The Government, by this one rupee an
acre, is repaid, more or less, for all outlay on repairing tanks
and other irrigation works.   It has been seen that the
Administration takes, besides, about a tenth or upwards of
nearly all the grain and rice crops raised by the capital, enterprise, and labour of the native cultivators.   In the 16 years
1868–83 this tenth land revenue amounted to 15,395,000 rupees,
while during the same period all other land revenues only
amounted to 1,512,000 rupees.

Import duties are as follows: on rice, wheat corn and
Indian corn, and other grain, 29 cents of a rupee (about $6\frac{1}{2}$d. a
bushel), on paddy (rice in the husk), 13 cents of a rupee.
Wheat flour, 1 rupee per cwt.   Dried fish, 50 cents per cwt.
Ghee, 2 rupees 50 cents per cwt.   Bacon, butter, ham, and

cheese, 3 rupees per cwt. Salted beef and pork, 1 rupee 25 cents per cwt. Tea, 25 cents per lb. Jaggery, or palm sugar, 50 cents; brown or muscovado sugar, 1 rupee 25 cents; and refined sugar, 2 rupees 50 cents per cwt. Salt, 2 rupees 13 cents per cwt. Cocoa-nut poonac, 25 cents per cwt. Pickles, sauces, confectionery, cocoas, 6$\frac{1}{2}$ per cent. *ad valorem*. Spirits under proof, 7s. 6d. per gallon, and in proportion to strength. Ale in wood, 3d. per gallon, and 7$\frac{1}{2}$d. per dozen. Wine in wood, 11$\frac{1}{4}$d. per gallon, and 1s. 5d. to 2s. per dozen. Tobacco, 2$\frac{1}{3}$d. per lb., unmanufactured; and 5$\frac{5}{8}$d. manufactured; 1s. 10$\frac{1}{2}$d. per lb. snuffs and cigars. The following articles pay 6$\frac{1}{2}$ per cent. *ad valorem* duty: candles, petroleum, pitch, vinegar, carriages, perfumery, stationery (except paper and envelopes, which are free), chemicals, soap, earthenware, glass and leather goods, clocks and watches, linseed and vegetable oils, hats and caps, gold and silver ware, starch, house furniture, linen, hempen and jute goods. Silks and woollens pay 6$\frac{1}{2}$ per cent., and cottons, 5 per cent. *ad valorem*. Pig iron pays 4s. 8$\frac{1}{4}$d. per ton; bars and rods, 7s. 6d. per ton; angle and Swedish, 9s. 4$\frac{1}{2}$d. per ton; corrugated, 13s. 1$\frac{1}{2}$d. per ton; galvanised roofing, 28s. 1$\frac{1}{2}$d. per ton; nails and rivets, 23s. 7$\frac{1}{2}$d. per ton; blister and cast steel, 18s. and 23s. 5$\frac{1}{2}$d. per ton. Lead, 11$\frac{1}{4}$d. per cwt. Zinc, in slabs, 11$\frac{1}{4}$d. per cwt.; perforated zinc, 5s. 7$\frac{1}{2}$d. per cwt. Brass and copper, 5s. 7$\frac{1}{2}$d. per cwt. Tin, 11$\frac{1}{4}$d. and 1s. 4$\frac{3}{4}$d. per cwt. Guns and rifles, 7s. 0$\frac{3}{8}$d. to 14s. 0$\frac{3}{4}$d. each; pistols, 4s. 2$\frac{5}{8}$d. to 8s. 5$\frac{1}{4}$d. each. Gunpowder, 5$\frac{5}{8}$d. a lb.; shot, 1s. 4$\frac{1}{8}$d. a cwt. Saltpetre refuse, not used in manure, 11$\frac{1}{4}$d. a cwt. Cement, 3$\frac{3}{4}$d. per cwt.

The exemptions are instructive: all machinery, railway iron, iron hooping and tanks, millwork, steam engines, bricks and tiles used in machinery buildings, manures, acids, fuller's earth, saltpetre refuse used in manure, mineral oils and grease, turpentine, rosin, coal and patent fuel, fire-clay, printing materials, mill and grinding stones, roofing slates, coil-yarn, rope, fibre, etc., horses, pianos, pictures, and gunny bags (to pack produce for export). A new industry has been introduced into Ceylon in recent years by the planters, because coffee was failing; this is the growth of tea. Tea is packed in lead, therefore tea-lead is now also exempted from duty. These exemptions have nothing to be said against them, but they embody the chief materials imported by planters for their business, and it contains few articles the people make any use of. The free village communities had evidently no hand in the framing of this list.

The spirit distilled in Ceylon, called "arrack," is manufactured by distillers who pay an annual licence of thirty rupees to Government. The number in 1883 was one hundred. The exclusive privilege of retailing this arrack is annually put up to auction in the several districts of the island. The renter is often the distiller also. The cost of the spirit, wholesale, is from seventy-five cents to one rupee a gallon, but the retailers are bound to sell it at a fixed rate, usually about three rupees to 3.50 rupees a gallon, sometimes more, as may be determined; taverns to sell arrack only pay no licence, but a general liquor shop has to pay 100 rupees. The Administration of the island is more than usually interested in the consumption of these spirituous liquors manufactured in it; it gains by the increased value of arrack farms (which show a steady rise). Combinations among arrack-renters have been known to endeavour to corner the Government and lower the selling price at auctions. In 1883 there were over 850 arrack-renters, about 140 liquor shopkeepers, and over 3,000 toddy-drawers in the island, besides distillers; but the Cingalees, from all accounts, are not an unsober race; some of the other races are not abstemious. Beer and porter only may be retailed on a ten rupees' licence, and the licence for selling intoxicants, not to be consumed on the premises, costs thirty rupees a year. The licence for liquors to be drunk on the premises costs 100 rupees a year. An hotel licence is 250 rupees.

The Ceylon system of licences is very searching, and comprises many industries, and the stamp duties are very elaborately set forth, and have been complained against for their irksomeness.

All servants must be registered, and sometimes the master, sometimes the servant, has to pay the charge, which is from a quarter rupee to half a rupee each time.

Timber may be cut in the Government forests (the Government owns all the forests) on paying a licence and 25 per cent. of the value of the timber. Jungle may be cut on payment of one-tenth, except in the northern province, where the charge is one-fifth of the estimated value. The quarries (in the western provinces) may be worked by payment of a royalty of 3 rupees 75 cents for every 1,000 stones, ·06 cents a cartload of cabook soil, and ·03 cents for sand. Dead chanks may be dug for on payment to Government of a fifth of their estimated value. The Government sells salt to the dealers at 2·36 cents per cwt.

The exclusive privilege of selling liquors distilled from palm-trees, and toddy generally, as well as the sale of arrack and rum, is farmed out in each province by Government.

There are certain tolls (a long list) collected on roads and bridges as well as for canals and ferries, and these are also rented or farmed out by the Government. For the local taxes in towns there is an assessment rate of 5 per cent. on property within the limits.

Matters are not always as quiet in Ceylon as they might be in administrative eyes. It appears that in some quarters of the island police are specially stationed, at the cost of the inhabitants accused of misconduct. This is an extreme measure, and the power to apply it ought not to be among the ordinary functions of an irresponsible administration. The cost of the administration of justice for the criminal classes is nearly £90,000 a year. There are between 1,600 and 1,700 regular police, costing about £60,000 a year.

The export duties are 200 rupees for each elephant, plumbago 25 cents per cwt., coffee and tea 5 cents per cwt., and cinchona 10 cents per cwt. The export duty on plumbago is virtually a royalty.

Wages for able-bodied daily field labour vary from 25 cents, or a fraction over 5½d., to 50 cents, or 11½d.; 7½d. a day is deemed good wages. Domestic labour is paid for at about the same rate. Other labour is paid, from unskilled at 3½d. per day, to 1s. 10½d. a day for skilled. Labourers are also engaged for periods, receiving at the rate of about 14s. a month, more being paid for special duties or exceptional capacity. Bread is said to be 5½d. per lb., flour being purchasable at from 33s. 9d. to 67s. 6d. the barrel of 196 lb. Bread is evidently not greatly in demand, for a barrel of flour can make 270 lb. The food of the people is rice, which may be bought cleaned at from 3s. 8d. to 5s. 7½d. the bushel; and in the husk, at from 1s. 8½d. to 1s. 11½d. the bushel. Beef sells from 3½d. to 5½d. per lb., and mutton from 5½d. to 11d., and pork at 5½d. Meat is cheap, but the quality is inferior.

A labouring man requires one bushel of rice a month in Ceylon (a native of Africa will want half as much again, at least); a man, wife, and three children will want at least three bushels a month—a total of thirty-six bushels a year for the family, costing for the lowest qualities perhaps 144s. The road tax will be 2s. 9¾d. for himself; the State taxes will be 8s. 6¼d. per head, or 42s. 7¼d. for the family; but as 19s. 6d. of this will have been included in the cost of the rice, the balance remaining to be paid will be only 23s. 1¼d. If a man be a good labourer, employed the whole year round, he will earn in 300 days, at 7½d. a day, 187s. 6d. After the above deductions, he will have 17s. 6¾d. left. But there will be some local tax, or forced labour, or bad weather, or illness, or all combined, to take something from his earnings, leaving him probably a balance of only 2s. or 3s., often nothing. He has yet to supply a home, clothing, and the various other essentials of the commonest existence. His wife and children will earn wages when competent to do so. In such cases the expenditure will also have to be greater for food necessaries. The greatest of mysteries in Eastern countries is how people manage to live. The official returns show that the population of Southern India earn less than 1d. a day per head; it used to be ½d. per day (their prosperity has recently doubled). Things are perhaps better in Ceylon, but life is dearer there also. It is of immense and paramount importance to look clearly into the minutest details of taxation and economic systems in such countries, for the ruin of a people is easily accomplished, their physical powers sapped, and their life-blood and vitality drained away from them for ever. The probability—the certainty, is that the people of Ceylon do not and cannot obtain or purchase enough food for a decent and healthy existence. The population do not live in these countries, they exist; and neither mental nor physical energy can ever be expected from them. It is melancholy to see travelled and instructed people speaking of these and similar races as being unfitted by Providence for those rights and duties which it is nevertheless certain the beneficent Creator intended all mankind equally to possess. A course of starvation extending over generations has had its depressing and demoralising results, and Nature is charged with giving birth to effeminate races when they are only a people suffering from the consequences of impolitic and oppressive economic systems. A food tax, however light, is the most unjust, as it is the most dangerous method by which revenue can be raised in such countries as Ceylon.

The mortgage laws are much complained of by parties interested in such matters, and they make out a strong case.

It is only in accordance with the strictest common sense that while people are disputing about property before a court of law, it should not meanwhile become valueless by the abandonment of all cultivation. In tropical countries, unless cultivation be kept up, a property, within a very short time, becomes a mere jungle. It may be necessary to go to a court of law to have a claim determined, but some method should be at hand to keep the property from deterioration or, may be, ruin.

The shipping returns show (for 1884) 3,294 vessels inwards, measuring 1,758,445 tons ; of these, 135 (steamers) measuring 217,490 tons, called at Colombo to coal, and 318 (steamers) measuring 432,731 tons, called at Galle. Of the above vessels 2,379, averaging 80½ tons each, were colonial coasters, and doing local trade with India and adjacent ports chiefly ; 745 were British, and averaged nearly 1,730 tons each ; 79 were French, averaging 1,955 tons each ; 37 were Austrian, averaging nearly 1,724 tons each ; and 10 were Italian, averaging 1,487 tons each. There was an increase of 76,082 tons in British shipping over the previous year, but there was a decrease of 20,058 tons in colonial shipping, and of 40,525 tons in foreign shipping. Most large steamers, British and foreign, on their way to and from China and the eastern ports, call at Ceylon, and this accounts for much of the above tonnage.

CHAPTER III.

MAURITIUS.

THE Island of Mauritius is much favoured by nature as regards soil, climate, and position. It is now essentially a sugar-growing colony, and its industrial existence practically depends on a profitable market being found for this commodity.

A lavish supply of capital, and a low-priced labour easily procurable, on conditions specially advantageous to planters, resulted in a forced production, and much of the resources of the island have been prematurely used up. A too great clearing of forest on an island of only about 700 square miles in extent, and far removed from any continent, has led to a lower rain-fall, and much of the old land is no longer cultivable with profit, while a still greater quantity has perceptibly deteriorated.

The newly cleared lands are wanted to take the place of abandoned or worn out districts which, if extreme caution be not used, are likely to increase in extent. The immense capital invested in this island is, some of it, in a precarious position, and it is important for all interests that the island should be placed on a more healthy and natural footing. Time and wise measures alone will bring this about.

The colony includes many smaller islands of value inhabited by mixed races. Some of these are fertile and some are renowned for their picturesqueness and the variety and rarity of their natural vegetable productions, but they are too small in extent to count for much as raisers of produce, and are, consequently, little heard of. One or two of them possess qualities which last, and are of more value for a power aiming at empire than the mere capacity to grow sugar. The harbour of Mahé, in the Seychelles Islands, has considerable capacity and splendid anchorages, and could be made anything of; the soft coral reefs are easily sawn, and capacious wharfs could be made; there is abundance of excellent water; the climate is warm, but healthy; there are no hurricanes, and it could be rendered as impregnable as Malta.*

Mauritius received a great blow by the opening of the Suez Canal, which diverted the valuable custom of a port of call, and for revictualling. The Canal had the same effect on its fortunes as a new line of railway would have had on a coaching inn in the olden days. The terrible fever epidemic of 1866 damaged its reputation as a sanatorium. Since these events it has become more than ever known as a sugar-growing colony, favoured by capitalists on account of the proximity of cheap coolie labour.

The population in 1883 was estimated to be about 361,000, of whom 246,600 were East Indians; about half of the latter are usually known by the denomination "coolie," which means a native of India hired by a planter to work at sugar-growing in some Crown colony for a term of years at a fixed tariff under the supervision of an official paid by the colony and nominated by the Colonial Office. A large number of these coolies elected to remain at Mauritius on the termination of

* Many excellent authorities prefer the position to that of Port Louis, Mauritius. The French, who are spending enormous sums in endeavouring to make harbours on the hurricane swept coast of Réunion, would give much for such a port, so situated.

their indentures, and continued to work on the estates as free labourers. The place suits them, on the whole, very well, and they thrive and some grow rich. They are a thrifty, painstaking, and frugal race; they are tenacious of all they get; all the lesser and a good deal of the higher commerce is falling into their hands; and much land is taken up by them directly as cultivators, and, indirectly, as mortgagees. Mauritius, unlike most other Crown colonies, had no aboriginal inhabitants. It was colonised by the French, whose language, customs, religion, and laws still predominate among the creoles. Up to the time of emancipation the land was cultivated by slaves from Madagascar and Africa, and since that period by coolies from India, who now with their descendants form the bulk of the population.

In the following calculations (taken from the Parliamentary returns and Blue Books) rupees are converted into sterling, at 2s. the rupee up to 1879; after that date the value has been usually calculated at 1s. 9d.

The exports from Mauritius have kept up well for the fifteen years ending 1883, without much variation in the value on the whole, but, as with the West Indian colonies, the quantity has, probably, been somewhat greater in recent years. The lower prices for sugar, the staple produce, have kept the exports from showing an increase.

The total exports for the five years, 1869–1873, were valued at £14,476,000 (2s. the rupee), an average of £2,895,000 a year. In the following six years, 1874–1879, they were valued at £20,051,000 (2s. the rupee), an average per year of £3,342,000. In the four years, 1880–1883, they came to 150,142,000 rupees, equal to £13,137,425 (at 1s. 9d. per rupee), an average of £3,284,000 a year.

The total imports for the five years, 1869–1873, were £11,101,000, an average of £2,220,000 a year. In the six years, 1874–1879, they were £14,037,000, an average of £2,340,000 a year. In the four years, 1880–1883, they were 102,145,000 rupees, equal to £8,937,687 (at 1s. 9d. per rupee), an average of £2,234,000 a year.

As with the exports, the imports into this colony have not increased in value during the last ten years. Of late years the rupee at Mauritius has been worth not over 1s. 8d. sterling. In the above period, 1869–1883, the total exports were valued at £47,665,000, and the total imports at £34,076,000,

showing an excess of the former over the latter to the large
amount of £13,589,000. · This is an average of over £900,000
a year, or, taking the fifteen years, the exports have exceeded
the imports by more than 50s. per head of population each
year.   The question that naturally arises will be, who receives
the equivalent for this?   The answer will be given farther on.
The exports to the United Kingdom for the five years ending
1873 average £897,000 a year, or nearly 31 per cent. of the
whole yearly exports; for the six years ending 1879, the
average was £1,010,000 a year, or a little over 30 per cent.;
and for the four years ending 1883 the average was £369,000
a year (at 1s. 9d. a rupee), or nearly 11¼ per cent. of the
exports of the colony for that period.

The imports from the United Kingdom for the five years
ending 1873 averaged £559,000 a year, a little over 25 per
cent. of total imports; for the six years ending 1879 the average had fallen to £490,000 a year, about 21 per cent.; for the
four years ending 1883 the average was £555,000 a year (at
1s. 9d. a rupee), about 25 per cent.

The Board of Trade returns give the value of exports from
the United Kingdom to Mauritius at about £569,000 or 7½
per cent. less than the colonial returns, and the imports to the
United Kingdom are valued at about £978,000, or 8⅛ per cent.
more than the colonial returns, for the fifteen years ending 1883.

Mauritius sends comparatively little produce to England;
her chief market is Australasia, to whose various ports she sent
upwards of 17½ millions sterling (at 2s. the rupee) of produce
in the fifteen years ending 1883.   She received in return, direct
from Australasia, less than 2 millions sterling, much of it in salted
beef and provisions.   This accounts for more than 15½ millions
of the 16 millions excess of exports over imports, referred to
before.   The produce shipped to Australasia was not paid for
in exports to Mauritius, but by bills and other arrangements
made by the owners, dealers, and shippers of the produce.
During the eight years 1869–76 Mauritius exported to the
Cape of Good Hope £540,000 in produce, and received
£331,000 in return.   In the seven years 1877–83 the shipment to the Cape largely increased, and amounted to
£1,732,000, the return imports amounting only to £343,000
in the seven years.   The shipments to the Cape exceeded the
imports from it by £1,598,000 (rupee 2s.) in the fifteen years,
The imports from France consist principally of wine, liquors.

millinery, haberdashery and apparel. In the eleven years
1869–79 Mauritius imported from that country goods valued
at £3,882,000 (2s. rupee), and exported to it only £1,400,000
in return. In the four years 1880–83 the imports from France
were valued at £1,555,000, and the exports to France at
£301,000 (at 1s. 9d. a rupee). The balance of this account,
amounting for the whole period of fifteen years to £3,736,000,
was probably settled in London. During the same period of
fifteen years, merchandise, valued at about £1,629,000 (2s. a
rupee), mostly guano and some mules, was imported from
Peru, and the payments for this amount were probably also
made in London, where are situated the chief offices of the
various companies who do most of the business of the island.
The Madagascar trade with Mauritius might have developed in
importance if recent events had not disturbed it. The total
imports (a good deal of them in live stock and straw bags for
sugar) for the fifteen years have been valued at £1,505,000,
and the exports to Madagascar at £1,511,000 (rupee 2s.), thus
balancing one another. The United States have recently
taken produce from Mauritius; in the four years 1880–83
the exports amounted to £553,000 (1s. 9d. the rupee), but
there were only about £20,000 in imports direct from the
United States for the same period. In the same four years
Mauritius imported from Pondicherry to the value of
£182,000, and exported direct in return only £58,000.

The trade with the adjoining French colony of Réunion, for
the three years 1881–83, amounted only to about £50,000 imports and £120,000 exports. There is a movement of trade
between Mauritius and the smaller islands of the colony valued
at about £50,000 a year imports and £38,000 a year exports.

The Seychelles Islands, until recently, were sadly neglected,
and indeed suffered serious injustice; there is even yet much to
be desired in their treatment. They are practically entirely
placed under the Mauritius Council, and as the supposed
interests of Mauritius are in some instances deemed not to be
identical with the interests of these islands as ports of call and
for other purposes, the laws and regulations enacted or permitted with respect to them have not always been framed with
that impartiality and strict fitness which should ever be the
standard of British administration. In order to please the
greater colony, where they lived and whose good report they
naturally valued most, and whose interests and even prejudices

they always warmly advocated and espoused, the Mauritius officials have ever thrown the weight of their opinion against these unfortunate islands, and were it not that the Secretary of State made it a rule that the Governors should occasionally visit them, so that they might see for themselves and redress some of their grievous wrongs, these islands to-day would be a discredit to the British Administration as they were some time back.

The imports of bullion and specie into Mauritius have decreased of late; in the 6 years ending 1875 they amounted to £1,639,000, of which £912,000 was re-exported; in the 7 years 1876–83 they were £1,732,000, the exports during the same period amounted to £940,000. It thus appears as if £1,619,000 remained in the islands; it is, indeed, estimated that 3,620,000 rupees are in the hands of the islanders, much of it being hoarded and concealed by Indians, and this would account for £316,750. The local banks would have a good deal, and much leaves the island without being declared at the custom house.

Mauritius imports food stuffs largely, mostly from India and Burmah. For the 17 years ending 1883, the average yearly value of rice, corn, and wheat imported into the island was over £645,000; £7,740,000 worth of rice alone was imported during that period. This is a large importation for a population numbering only 361,000 in 1883. The importance of the above imports of grain food may be estimated from the fact that during the same term of 17 years the average importation of cottons, haberdashery, and millinery combined averaged £220,000 a year, or only a little over a third in value of the former. The total imports into Mauritius from India (including bullion and specie) for the 10 years ending 1883, were valued at £9,071,000 sterling (2s. a rupee).

During the 17 years ending 1883, this colony imported on an average machinery and mill-work to the amount of £39,000 a year. In 1883, the quantity imported from the United Kingdom was valued at 510,000 rupees, and from Belgium and France at 522,000 rupees. Cutlery and hardware to the value of about £61,000 a year was imported during the same period, mostly from the United Kingdom. Out of £805,000 cotton goods imported in the 5 years, 1879–1883, the United Kingdom sent only £122,000.

The revenue raised during the 10 years, 1871–1880, was

£7,238,796 (the rupee throughout estimated at 2s. sterling) of which £2,252,701, or about 31 per cent., was raised by custom duties. During the last 3 years the revenue raised by Government was 26,258,200 rupees, equal to about rupees 24·$\frac{33}{100}$ per head of population.

The average wages of the working classes in tropical agricultural colonies subject to the system of coolie labour, or practically depending on it for the production of its exportable produce, is necessarily low, because such labour is regulated by contract for a term of years, at a price for which independent labour, when procurable, usually refuses to work, or, which amounts to the same thing, at a price and on conditions which make independent labour unreliable. According to the *Mauritius Mercantile and Commercial Gazette*, 16th February, 1885, the wages of Indians—1st and 2nd class best labourers— have been reduced to 5 or 6 rupees a month, and rations reduced as low as possible, salaries of sirdars and all employés being similarly lowered.

The public taxes are levied on a system assumed to be in harmony with public opinion. It might be deemed unnecessary to inquire too minutely into the formation of this opinion, and into its authority; but experience of Crown colonies, and an examination of their tariffs, leads one to doubt on these matters. In every country, whether free or dependent, personal interest and personal claims are always the most aggressive, and every one is ready in the public interest to place burdens on other people's shoulders. In the Mauritius, as in the West Indies, the statement is made with apparent conviction as to its soundness, that the only way to get the idle man (the man who will not work for the planter on the conditions offered) to pay any taxes, is to levy a rate on imported food. And the industrious labourer with a family, who practically is the chief consumer of the article, has to suffer, in order that this statesman-like and quasi fair play policy may be carried on. But the fact is the tax is not imposed or maintained for such reasons, nor would it be proper or possible that it should be so; if the tax on rice and grain be otherwise an impolitic tax it should be done away with, if it be sound in principle on other grounds, and levied fairly, let it remain; but let not the idle man be falsely deemed indirectly the means of shaping the fiscal policy of the colony. Then what is the public opinion that upholds these taxes? It is the opinion of the few who do not feel them; of the few who cannot trace their evil effects on the welfare of the many, and on the industry of the place; they are kept up in the interests of the few who fear their abolition will ultimately lead to a burden falling on their own shoulders. These are the reasons for the continuation of the system.   The labourer pays duty on the clothes he wears, the same as the rich man, and no less; he pays as much on his spirits as the rich man on his imported wine and beer; and nearly as much on his leaf tobacco as the other on his manufactured tobacco and cigars; and he pays quite enough by this and other ways. A place, an island, far away by itself in the Indian Ocean, levying a tax upon an article of importation such as rice, on which its existence depends (if the supply were to fail to come for a single year the place would starve outright) seems impolitic, especially when the tax may very well be replaced by others more safe and more equitable.

The customs charges are 54 cents of a rupee on every 100 kilogrammes of grain, dholl, lentils, rice, and wheat; 60 cents the 100 kilos of maize; and 80 cents the 100 kilos of beans, barley, oats, peas, and wheat flour. In 1883 rice was imported valued at 3,177,279 rupees, the duty was 300,809 rupees, being $9\frac{1}{2}$ per cent. on the declared value. The rice was nearly all from India, where another duty equal to $6\frac{1}{8}$d. per cwt., or about 8 per cent. on its value, on the spot, was charged on its export—a total of $17\frac{1}{2}$ per cent. on its value. During the same year the imports of grain, oats, maize, barly, dholl, lentils, peas and wheat were valued 1,814,683 rupees. Most of these articles were also from India, but there were no charges made on them in that country. The duties of entry into Mauritius amounted to 170,816 rupees, over $9\frac{1}{4}$ per cent. on the declared value. Wheat flour is chiefly imported from Australasia, in casks, the quantity imported in 1883 was valued at 732,747 rupees, on which a duty amounting to 31,804 rupees, or $4\frac{1}{3}$ per cent. only on its declared value was levied. Wheat flour is the food of the rich and the well to do; it therefore has to pay less than half the duty that is charged on rice and the other grain foods consumed by the working classes. Such is the public voice that regulates taxation in this island. The other duties levied are as follows :—4 rupees on every 100 kilogrammes of butter, cheese, coffee, refined sugar, bacon, ham, tongue, sausages, &c. This will be about 4s. $5\frac{1}{2}$d. a cwt. The duties on beef, pork, biscuits, and ships' bread is 2 rupees the 100 kilogrammes or 2s. 2¾d. a cwt. The duty on fish dried and salted is 1 rupee the 100 kilos., or 1s. 1⅜d. a cwt. To show how an apparently low specific duty can influence the cost of a low-priced article it will be only necessary to point out that in 1883 dried fish was imported, chiefly from the Cape of Good Hope, valued at 391,395 rupees, and the duty levied on it at Mauritius came to 24,310 rupees, or nearly 6¼ per cent. on its declared import value.

The duty on colonial spirits is $9\frac{60}{100}$ rupees the decalitre, sweetened spirits being charged $6\frac{60}{100}$ rupees extra (the duty paid on rum for home consumption in 1883 amounted to the large sum of 1,772,354 rupees). Ale is charged 7 rupees the hectolitre (about 7½d. a gallon), and 1 rupee the dozen bottles. The duty on wine (the quantity imported is considerable) is about 8¼d. a gallon in the wood and 2s. the dozen litres. Tea is charged only 1d. a pound. Unmanufactured tobacco is 1s. 5d. a pound, manufactured tobacco 1s. 9¼d. a pound, and cigars 1s. 11d. a pound. Cottons, silks, woollens, linens pay 6¾ per cent. *ad valorem ;* also all iron, glass, and earthenware, leather, oils, candles, soap and salt. Paper, stationery and books enter free.

The other chief articles exempted from duty are machinery, manures, and coals; very good exemptions, but, nevertheless, class exemptions.

There is an export duty on sugar, the produce of the colony, of 4½d. a cwt. (30 cents per 100 kilos.), which in 1883 realised 347,380 rupees. There was even a surcharge during the year on this duty, realising 81,055 rupees. The abolition of this duty was lately under consideration, and it has, perhaps, been done away with.

The local taxes are far-reaching ; every business, profession, and trade imaginable has to pay a yearly licence. In 1883 the shops paid 604,604 rupees, common hawkers 53,845 rupees, fishermen 4,644 rupees, professions 25,281 rupees. There are game licences, of course, and licences for hotels and coffee-houses, and the like ; and on carriages, horses, and so on.

The railways belong to Government, the yearly traffic receipts are from 1½ million to 1¾ million. The debenture debt on the 31st December, 1883, was £753,500.

Taking the general trade of the island, it has been seen that only about one-quarter of the imports, and 11¼ per cent. of the exports, are with the United Kingdom. There is a

E

large intercolonial trade with India, Australia, and the Cape of Good Hope. The imported cottons are partly from the United Kingdom, but there is a large importation from India. France does most of the hosiery trade, the bulk of the haberdashery trade, and all the boot and shoe trade. The imports of earthenware, chinaware, glassware, and hardware are divided between Great Britain, France, and Germany; Great Britain doing the most.

In the year 1883, 513 vessels, measuring 301,508 tons, entered with cargo, and 64 vessels, measuring 28,904 tons, in ballast. Of these, 309 vessels, measuring 168,195 tons, were British, and 140 vessels, 119,549 tons, were French. It must be understood that the steam communication of Mauritius and Seychelles with Europe and India, _viâ_ Aden, is carried on by the great French Company, the "Messageries Maritimes," subsidised by the French Government for the sake of the neighbouring French colony of Réunion; the steamers are monthly, and their termini are Mauritius and Aden.

In the eighteen years, 1866–1883, Mauritius exported about two million tons of sugar, being, during that period, about 31 per cent. of the total exports of the sugar-producing colonies of the United Kingdom (exclusive of India; but this country exports comparatively little of the £22,000,000 of sugar computed to be annually grown). British Guiana now produces about as much sugar as Mauritius. In the year 1883 the import of cane sugar from Mauritius into the United Kingdom was only about $2\frac{1}{2}$ per cent. of the whole of that description of sugar imported, and $12\frac{1}{2}$ per cent. of the produce of the island for the year. Mauritius, like other British colonies, sends her produce to other markets when convenient for her to do so.

The inhabitants of inter-tropical lands, such as Mauritius, should be indeed rich; Nature does so much. In 1883 the exports nearly reached 105 rupees per head of population, the imports were nearly 74 rupees per head. But Mauritius is not nearly so rich a place as it should be. It is well off no doubt compared to a West India island. The laws, especially the land laws, enable land to be held and cultivated by the people. The succession laws are just. The mortgage laws secure to the lender, whoever he may be, the amount he advances; he runs the ordinary risks of depreciation, but no one can take away and pocket the advances he has made on the land as may be done, according to law in the West Indies, by the "Consignee." The coolie being the only labourer, the great injustice done to Jamaica and other West Indian islands by his introduction does not operate.

It is to be hoped the new constitution given, or about to be given, to the people of this island will prove not only a blessing to them, but to many; for according to the uses they make of the new powers given them will it be judged wise or the reverse to give the like to others. The chances are greater in Mauritius than in the West Indies that the separate interests of all classes and races will coalesce for the common good. The genuine friends of Crown colonists, and the real lovers of liberty and freedom everywhere, have been often adverse to granting full rights of self-government, because the franchise in such cases has so often been held and exercised by a certain class only, with the result of imposing an intolerable tyranny on the remainder of the population. If an elective body be not constituted so as to include all classes and all interests, better almost for those excluded to have none. It is often said that Eastern people prefer a despotic government; they have not had many chances of an alternative choice; but, perhaps, they would prefer it, on the whole, to an oligarchy; and, above all, to that meanest and most depressing of all tyrannies, an oligarchy of absentee planters. When politicians propose measures, the reasons they publicly give for them are those only which are intended to meet apprehended opposition, the objects really aimed at are often carefully hidden; but there is no doubt it is intended that Mauritius should enter the path of self-government. There were somewhat similar measures proposed by certain parties for some West Indian islands, but they were not identical in the objects aimed at. What the people in the Crown colonies really want is to be governed as little as possible, to be able to live on their own land without being too much worried and meddled with by regulations and laws, to impose their own taxes, to have good cheap food, and, above all, to enjoy their earnings themselves.

CHAPTER IV.

FIJI.

THERE was an opportunity lost at Fiji. The import tariffs established in that colony are elaborate and severe ; they bear a strong likeness to those in some other Crown colonies, noted for their onerous customs duties, and in many points they can, unfortunately, be compared with the restrictive tariffs so much complained of in some of the neighbouring Australian colonies. There is one great exception in their favour ; wheaten flour is permitted to enter free of duty. It is not very evident why this useful article should be so favoured (unless it be. .to encourage flour imports from Australia), while corn flour, maizena, oatmeal, and biscuits, should be charged 1d. per lb., and rice 10s. a ton. The latter articles should enter somewhat largely into the food of the people. It is well to encourage the consumption of every form of flour food ; the higher the class of food commonly used, the more civilised, industrious, and self-respecting will be the people. Not only wheaten flour, but rice and corn flour, and, indeed, every description of flour and grain, should be free from duties of customs.

The following are the chief tariffs :—Biscuits, barley, corn flour, maizena, oatmeal, split peas, sugar, sago, jams and jellies, and candles, pay 1d. per lb. ; malt and oats, 6d. a bushel ; tea, coffee, chicory, cocoa, chocolate, and macaronis, 3d. per lb. ; common soap ½d. per lb., or 22 per cent. on its cost ; fancy soap, 15 per cent. *ad valorem ;* bacon, cheese, dates, dried and preserved fruits, hams and cured pork, 2d. per lb ; unmanufactured tobacco, 1s. per lb. ; manufactured tobacco, 3s. per lb. ; cigars and cigarettes, 5s. per lb. ; ale, &c., 1s. a gallon in bottles, and 9d. a gallon in wood ; wine, in wood, 2s. to 4s. a gallon, and in bottles, 4s. to 12s. a gallon ; spirits, 12s. a gallon ; opium, 15s. per lb. ; salt and Scotch soda, 20s. a ton ; butter, Indian and other corn, 5 per cent. *ad valorem ;* potted meats, pickled and dried fish, drapery, earthenware, drugs, boots and shoes, glassware, furniture, carriages, clocks, ironmongery, nails, iron tanks, sauces, and oilman's stores 10 per cent. *ad valorem.* 15 per cent. is charged on perfumery, and 20 per cent. on jewellery and fire-arms. Iron in bars, &c., pays 20s. a ton, and galvanised iron 40s. a ton. Kerosene oil is charged 6d. a gallon ; sporting powder 6d. per lb. ; paper pays

3s. per cwt., and for stationery purposes 10 per cent. *ad valorem*. Wheaten flour, iron rails, preserved and salted meat (an Australian import) and machinery, are free.

There is an export duty of £5 per ton on sandal-wood, and 2½ per cent. on silver coin when over £10. The Western Australian export duty on sandal-wood is only 5s. a ton; if there was any business to be done at Fiji with this article, the difference would be serious. Perhaps this high export duty is intended to limit the export.

In 1881 the population numbered 124,788 (natives, immigrants, and mixed races) and 2,307 Europeans. In the Island of Rotumah the population was 2,500. The area of the colony is something over 8,000 square miles.

The total imports for the six years 1875–80 were valued at £810,871, and for the three years 1881–3, £1,030,000. The total exports for the six years 1875 80 were £930,000, and for the three years 1881–3 £715,000.

Like most British tropical Crown colonies, Fiji is anxious to enter the race to provide the already rather lavishly supplied sugar market. During the five years 1878–82 she exported 4,350 tons of sugar, she shipped about 5,000 tons in 1883, but it did not go to England.

Fiji takes few goods from the United Kingdom except machinery and iron-work. In the four years 1879 83 about 21½ per cent. of her imports were from Great Britain, and 73 per cent. of these consisted of metals, machinery, and mill-work. In the five years 1879–83 she sent 18½ per cent. of her exports to the United Kingdom, consisting chiefly of substances from which oil is to be expressed. Some of the declared exports of Fiji consist of cotton and copra imported from Samoa; these amounted to £27,000 in 1883. There is a considerable export of green fruit, valued at £15,500 in 1883. The main industry is the preparation and export of copra; this amounted to 6,203 tons in 1883, valued at £80,647. The trade of Fiji is almost entirely with Australasia. In 1883, 198 vessels entered these islands, having an average of 346 tons each; 159 were under British colours, with an average of 355 tons each.

The revenue for the four years 1878–81 was £297,000, of which £89,000 was raised by customs. The revenue for the two years 1882–83 was £218,000, of which £83,000 was raised by customs; in the last two years the customs revenue was 38

per cent of the whole, in the previous four years it was about
29¾ per cent. of the whole. The nature of the customs charges
have been already referred to. The internal taxation, in one
direction, is wide and exhaustive ; every person who purposes
to carry on any industry or trade has to pay a special tax for
the permission to do so. A baker in a town has to pay £3,
and in the country £1 ; a butcher in a town has to pay £10 ;
a chemist, £20 ; joint stock company agents are charged £25.
Even a hawker has to pay £2. Land surveyors are charged
£5. A wholesale store pays £15 in a town, £10 in the
country ; and a retail store with a hawker's business in the
country will have to pay £4. Publicans in a town are charged
£45, and in the country £15. No one is exempted ; a barber
pays £2, a carpenter £5, a shoemaker, £2, a tailor £2, and
so on, by the year. Marriage registrations, £1.

The public debt is £250,000.

This colony has not yet settled down into a fixed condition.
There remain many weighty problems still to be settled, and it
will be some time before they are all solved. The people are
in a transition state, and, naturally, they must be governed in
many matters by their old customs and laws until circumstances
arise when alterations may become advisable and practicable.
It is admitted by all competent authorities that the Administration has acted, so far, with foresight and discretion in dealing
with the natives. It is difficult for civilised governments to
deal justly with primitive communities, because they have not
the courage to restrain their subjects from taking those unfair
advantages which even the commonest and dullest of civilised
men have over the shrewdest of savages. There are not wanting those who look on the extermination of savage races as a
benefit. But experience, scientific research, and history all
prove, every day more and more, that such conclusions are mis-
taken. Civilised people know something, but not much, about
their own intelligence, and they know something of their own
history, but they know nothing whatever about these people
they condemn to extinction simply because they do not understand them. Savages are, in fact, easier to be taught than civilised men ; it is easier for them to break with the past. As
Principal Fairbairn said in the *Contemporary Review*, March,
1884, " there is less of hope of a debased civilisation than of
the rudest and frankest naturalism." It is to be hoped many
races will survive in the world, were it only to avoid too much

monotony. In his work, "Man before Metals," Mr. N. Joly says : " The instincts common to all humanity necessarily produce a similarity of results when men are subjected to the same needs, and placed in the same circumstances." The fundamental passions and morals of mankind are eternally the same ; it is only manners that vary. The extinction of races in such places as Fiji only result in the after letting in of some well-known type of no particular interest, and perhaps of less real capacity. It is to be hoped Fiji will escape for some time yet from the condition Mr. Leroy-Beaulieu so well expresses by the term, "Glorification of exports :" "*Le régime artificiel avait fondé nos colonies sur la servitude, sur le monopole, sur le commerce extérieur ; il en était resulté la glorification presque exclusive des produits d'exportation et principalement de la canne ; un tel ordre de choses a fait son temps.*" It is to be feared, however, that the system is not yet quite exploded.

CHAPTER V.

MALTA.

THE natives of this small island are noted in the many places where they are found for their industrial qualities ; they are a frugal and hard-working people, painstaking in all they undertake and persevering in their objects. Education leaves something to be desired, otherwise, in a position so open to the world and so much visited, one would expect to see fewer prejudices and more of that industrial, economical, and commercial tact and knowledge which has made the fortune and reputation of many places less favoured by position in the Mediterranean and other seas. The Maltese, it is true, are renowned as successful petty traders, and have made a reputation in certain callings and industries they almost may claim as their own, but these qualities do not suffice, of themselves, to create a great commercial centre. When the vested interests of a powerful class are involved in any established system, it is of little use endeavouring to remodel or alter it, however mischievous it may be, unless other interests equally strong and powerful, if not more so, are on the spot to insist on a change. This is the reason, and the only one, why protection flourishes

anywhere.   What can be more difficult than the getting rid of
an obnoxious tax when there is no public opinion of sufficient
political potency on the spot to urge the administration into
action ?   The high duties on grain in Malta have had more evil
results for the people of the United Kingdom than many grave
calamities.   The people and the merchant mariners of adjacent
countries may hear much of British policy, but they can see for
themselves that in the British colony of Malta protection in its
worst form is maintained, and it is not unreasonable for them to
argue that when the British Foreign Office and British commercial agents urge the advantages of free trade they are not
acting consistently; a suspicion would be aroused that the
fiscal policy so much vaunted must have something against it,
when the people who talk so loudly in its favour allow their
Crown colonies to so heavily tax, as to almost exclude, the
grain and flour of their neighbours.   Neither has the tax in any
measure benefited Malta; half the sad diseases in the island
are known to be due to the low-class diet of the labouring
population.   It is said the people of the island oppose the free
introduction of grain, not because they have too much for their
own use—which is not the fact by a long way—but because
such introduction would endanger the not too great profits now
obtained by its cultivation.   Yes ! the growers of grain must be
supported, even at the cost of the physical health of the people,
and the children of the humble must remain ill-fed in order that
certain proprietors may effect a satisfactory balance sheet.
How would they like the English people to act on the same
principle, and exclude the 107,000 cwt. of potatoes they sent to
the United Kingdom in 1883?   The proprietors of Malta
would do better to grow those crops which require no bolster-
ing, and not to have the starving poor to contribute their mites
to their income.   It is conceivable the military governors of
Malta should not have been very zealous in this matter. The
position of Malta is so unique and excellent that the trade of
its chief port is even now considerable, and were it a free
port, this might become so extended as to interfere with its
position and *status* as a military stronghold.

In most Crown colonies the two opposing influences
of free trade and protection are struggling for the upper
hand, and the former has by no means always on its side
the local Government authorities.   On the whole, the Crown
colonies have not, with some notable exceptions, been al-

together unfortunate in the contest. The sympathies of the people of the United Kingdom in this matter happen to coincide with their material interests, but under any circumstances they would be on the side of the people of the colonies struggling against those who favour high tariffs, either for protectionist or for revenue purposes. But it has been seen how the interests of a class of local cultivators, the desire of others to shift the chief burden of taxation from their own shoulders on to those of the consuming public and the labouring classes, who have no voice in the matter, and the satisfaction of the colonial executives at having a form of taxation by which they avoid immediate contact with the contributors, all combine to keep up a system in the Crown colonies that has been condemned at home as unjust and impolitic.

The revenue for 10 years, 1874–83, amounted to £1,857,000, of which no less a sum than £1,066,000 was raised by duties of customs. In 1884, the revenue was £212,569, the share of duties of customs being £119,080, During the same year the population of all the islands was deemed to be 156,675 (153,812 Maltese, 1801 United Kingdom, 1062 foreign), the taxation per head will therefore be a little under 27s. 2d. Considering the nature of the population, the average earnings of labour, and, above all, the form in which the revenue is raised, most people will think it sufficient.

The Maltese tariff is 10s. per strike salm for wheat, 6s. for Indian corn, 4s. for barley, 3s. to 5s. for other grains. Manufactured grain pays 6s. per cantar; damaged grain, unfit for food, 2s. the salm; pulse and seeds pay 2s. 6d. per salm; olive oil pays 6d. per caffiso. Spirits are charged 22s. to 24s. 2d. the Maltese barrel, wine and ale also pay a duty. Tobacco and all other articles are free. There is a revenue from land (it came to nearly £15,000 in 1884), and there are other rents (worth over £23,000 in 1884). There are licences and dividends, and there was an imperial grant in 1884 of £10,000 for maintenance of Egyptian and other refugees.

Malta shows a very large total for imports and exports, but nearly all of the produce and merchandise included in them simply entered the harbour for a time, and then cleared out in the same bottom, to proceed to the destination intended. This traffic is almost entirely with steamers. Out of 3,278 British vessels which entered in 1884 only 14 were sailing vessels; out of 290 vessels under foreign (European) flags—not including Italy and Turkey—only 13 were sailing vessels. With Italy and Turkey it is different, the Italians had 978 sailing vessels to 133 steamers, and the Turkish flag 60 sailing vessels to 19 steamers. The imports for 1884 were valued at £13,343,789, but only merchandise valued at £634,744 was landed, the balance (£12,709,045) went on its way. Much of the merchandise landed at Malta is subsequently re-exported.

In the 5 years, 1879–83, the Board of Trade returns show importations into the United Kingdom from Malta and Gozo valued at £863,000, of which £324,000 was for potatoes and onions. The exports to Malta and Gozo of the produce and manufactures of the United Kingdom were valued at £4,522,000, of which about £2,000,000 was for wearing apparel and haberdashery, cottons, linens, and woollens. £1,180,000 for coal and fuel, and £277,000 for sugar refined in the United Kingdom ; much of this was for sale to passing vessels and for re-export.

The imports of British beer and ale into Malta are considerable ; in the 5 years these amounted to £211,000. Among articles of foreign and colonial produce and manufactures imported from the United Kingdom in the 5 years, the most prominent were coffee (£229,000), rice (100,000), sugar (£137,000), and tobacco (£133,000). Much of the provisions will be for the supply of the large garrison. The total exports to Malta from the United Kingdom of foreign and colonial produce and manufactures were valued at £932,000 for the 5 years 1879–83.

CHAPTER VI.

WEST AFRICA.

OF all the colonial possessions of the British Crown, the most disappointing have undoubtedly been the territories and protectorates in Western Africa. Time out of mind great expectations have been formed of them, expeditions after expeditions have been undertaken, numerous wars have been fought, and all of them have been gloriously concluded, treaties have been made of the most satisfactory and binding character, the despatches of governors have shown the most splendid results of an astute and far-seeing diplomacy, territories have been annexed and settlements founded, and large sums have been spent by the British Government in various ways, and in the latter half of the year 1885, the actual position, on the whole, looks wonderfully like what it was at any previous time during the last twenty or fifty years, or before. British administration in Western Africa has not been a success.

It must have been a failure ; the elements necessary for the most temporary success have always been wanting. It is difficult at any time to rule a country against the wish of its inhabitants ; but the West African system has been, as much as possible, to rule the country as if there were no inhabitants in it. They have been acknowledged to exist, it is true, in treaties, in wars, and in expeditions, and they must have been supposed to exist for taxing purposes ; for few, if any other, reasons have been given for recent annexations, except the necessities of the custom houses, or the fear of other nations placing rival custom houses too near them.

British rule in Western Africa should be an unmixed benefit to the people, and of immense value to British commerce ; but in order to accomplish this the presence of the people must be acknowledged, and their co-operation enlisted in the good work. It is possible that the various settlements within the strict limits of their legal boundaries may have been managed, on the whole, as well as circumstances admitted from the usual point of view of Crown colonies; but British power and political influence have never been confined to these limits in Western Africa, nor have they ever pretended to be so. When a long line of coast has been declared British territory by the usual methods employed on such occasions, and custom houses and revenue officials hold sway over it, all native rule is destroyed for a considerable distance inland. Now it so happens that in such cases a reign of murder, plunder, and general disorganisation ensues in these hapless lands, and no one is held responsible. The British administration adheres to its strict limits, or to its supposed limits, under shelter of its forts and fleets, and takes no heed of its solvent influence over native rule, which falls to pieces by mere proximity. It is curious to note how little heed is taken of the rights of other and contiguous people by local administrations ; and it is not too much to say that almost all wars, disputes, heart-burnings, and troubles on the coast adjacent to the British settlements are entirely and solely due to this selfish and unpardonable oversight and deliberate injustice. The only system known in Africa for raising revenue is by duties of customs, either on exports or imports; and when a European power annexes a line of coast, it practically commands the revenue of the whole country supplied by that line of coast. To take possession of a mere fringe of coast, as Great Britain has often done, and to refuse all responsibilities of government beyond that fringe is manifestly an unjust proceeding, because the inland people are thereby equally taxed with those on the coast, and probably more so from having no facilities for smuggling, and the inland chiefs chafe under a taxation for which neither they nor their people receive any equivalent whatever. In the five years ending 1883, the revenue raised in the four British West African settlements (Gambia, Sierra Leone, Gold Coast, and Lagos) amounted to £1,253,000, of which £1,016,300 was raised by duties of customs.

If British dominion in Africa should ever be of any real good to the people, or of any lasting benefit to British commerce, it will only be by an entire reversal of the policy so long pursued. The various settlements should be looked upon only as stations or convenient outposts for opening up the interior portions of the vast continent to the advantages of commerce and industry, without which neither civilisation nor Christianity itself can make any headway in these lands. No attempt even should be made to govern the country anywhere except through the selected chiefs of the people, who are open to the best influences, and whom the people will implicitly obey. A noble career lies before any European people whose executive adopts this simple method of dealing with a great and much-wronged race. British dominion in various forms has. been established in portions of this western coast for two centuries and upwards, and there is more than enough experience to prove that white men can never inhabit it except in small numbers and at perpetual risk of life. In fact the country must be ruled and governed by a native element, and Great Britain can easily assist and guide it by laws and regulations—the fruit of ages of experience—engrafted on to and merged with such existing native systems and methods the people may desire to keep to and to follow.

The actual British possessions, as such, have been of no value to the United Kingdom, and they have conferred no benefit on the African race; and it is much open to doubt whether, if they had never existed, civilisation and Christianity would not have made more way among the people. Such is the result of a narrow policy around which, on four isolated spots on the coast, have grown up four small communities of Crown colonists, having no sympathy or touch with the large populations and rich countries of the near interior, and they are unknown beyond.

As might be expected from what has been said above, the trade of these four settlements is inexpansive and irregular. They have all had their movements, usually short-lived, when trade blossomed and the frontiers were quiet, and then follow the dark hours of trouble, and loss and bloodshed and reprisals. It is a sorrowful history, ending to-day as it began over two centuries ago, monotonous in its gloom and sad in its disappointments; and so it will continue, and the same tale will ever have to be told until the machine be lifted out of the rut in which it has so long stagnated. As Sir Thomas Brassey has well said in his work, "Foreign Work and English Wages," under head "Colonisation" :—We cannot create a trade with Africa or New Guinea without first raising those countries in the scale of nations. We must co-operate with the native populations in the development of their resources, we must help them to accumulate wealth, or they cannot purchase our goods."

The total exports of British West Africa for the seven years, 1867–73, were £9,274,000, an average of £1,325,000 a year; for the following seven years, 1874-80, they were £10,715,000, an average of £1,530,000 a year; for the three years, 1881–83, they were £4,543,000, an average of £1,514,000 a year. Taking similar periods, the imports for the seven years, 1864–73, were £7,245,000, an average of £1,035,000 a year; for the seven years, 1874–80, they were £9,563,000, an average of £1,366,000 a year; and for the three years, 1881–83, they were £4,192,000, an average of £1,397,000 a year. The total exports for the eighteen years were, £24,532,000; and the total imports, £21,000,000. It must be understood, of course, that most of the produce exported by way of the British ports is not obtained in the settlements, but in the adjacent countries. In the same way most of the imports go to pay for the produce thus obtained.

Most of the gold exported from West Africa is from the Gold Coast, but some finds its way from the interior to the other settlements. Since the introduction of the palm oil industry on the Gold Coast, the people occupy themselves more profitably in collecting the valuable berries from the vast palm oil tree forests, and preparing the oil and kernels for conveyance by human porterage—by land—and by water to the coast towns, than by seeking for gold. The gold exported from the Gold Coast in 1883 was valued at £52,435, all of which, with the exception of £373, was sent to the United Kingdom. The exports of bullion and specie from British West Africa in the four years, 1880–83, were valued at £394,792 ; and the imports of bullion and specie for the same period were valued at £335,275, the latter mostly consisting of newly-coined silver from Great Britain.

A large quantity of rice is grown in the neighbourhood of the Sierra Leone possessions and southwards, the tribes ·or nations in those parts subsisting largely on this produce. This native-grown rice is of a very superior quality to any imported ; it is not only cultivated on the plains adjoining the large rivers, which are flooded every year the same as the valley of the Nile, but on the slopes and hill-sides. Nevertheless, over 10,000 tons of cleaned rice were imported into Sierra Leone ports in the five years, 1879–83 ; nearly all this rice was from India and Burmah, *via* Great Britain. On the Gold Coast and the adjoining countries rice is practically unknown to the people. Here maize is the national diet, and is consumed in the form of a fermented paste ; no rice, in consequence, is imported into this country, but the Americans do a considerable and growing trade in flour and biscuits. Those whose only opportunities have been to observe the people of the coast, and especially the people of the British settlements, whose physique has degenerated through the unwholesomeness of the positions even for Africans, and the imperfect sanitary arrangements and want of water, and also from a large consumption of the vilest imported liquors misnamed rum and gin, can have but a very inadequate opinion of the capacities of the African race. The British policy so long pursued has confined direct European trade and intercourse to the swampy fringe of coast, leaving the interior untouched. The African is destined to be one of the strongest races in the world, physically, as well as one of the most influential; he will be dominant in his own huge continent of Africa and have something to say in America. No one who has observed the African at home (not including

Sierra Leone and the British coast towns, for reasons before given), and in the West Indies, but must be immediately struck at the enormous physical degeneracy of the race at the latter place. In Africa food is abundant in the shape of the best rice, corn, and oil seeds; and, besides, there are no duties on the entry of food. In the British West Indies the people have been pauperised, home-grown food is scarce, and is inferior in quality to the African descriptions, and a crushing duty is imposed on every description of imported food. Food duties are not only administratively impolitic and commercially unsound, but they are cruel to the people.

The imports of United Kingdom goods only, into British West Africa for the seven years 1867–73 averaged £668,000 a year; in the following seven years (1874–80) the yearly average was £934,000, in the three years 1881–83 the average was £764,000 a year. The increase of these imports during the last ten years has not been due to any greater trade with the United Kingdom; it is due to the fact that the trade with the Dutch settlements since their annexation to the British Gold Coast has been transferred from the heading "Trade with Foreign Countries and their Possessions" to "Trade with British Possessions."

The possessions of foreign powers in Western Africa during the five years 1879–83 imported from the United Kingdom merchandise of the average annual value of £312,000, of which £293,000 were exclusively British goods, the remainder consisting, mainly, of rice and other products from British India and colonies. Those territories which, until recently, might have been designated Native, or Independent Western Africa, but much of which have lately found new masters in Germany and Great Britain, imported merchandise from the United Kingdom of the average value of £1,080,000 a year for the five years 1879-83, of which £872,400 a year were exclusively British goods. The importation into West Africa of foreign merchandise *via* England is probably profitable to the British merchants engaged; it consisted in rice, £19,000 a year (probably chiefly from India); £85,000 a year in tobacco, chiefly from the United States; arms, £12,000 a year, chiefly from Germany; beads, £15,000 a year, a good deal of which are from Venice; and spirits £25,000 a year, chiefly from Hamburg (a vile stuff, much of it distilled from wood and sawdust). Germany has made great efforts to produce, at a low cost, articles readily saleable in the markets of backward countries ; red calicoes, Saxony prints, Hagan hardware, and gunpowder, are finding an increased market, and even "articles de Paris," which have a not inconsiderable sale in West Africa, are being supplanted by German goods. Were German manufacturers unfettered at home, and the incubus of protection removed from them, they would be the most formidable of competitors for the trade of the world in every branch of industry.

The settlements at the Gambia River charge only a duty of 2 per cent. *ad valorem* on ordinary merchandise, and food is free. The only objection is the large and unexplained charge of 1d. per lb. on all sugar. There is a duty charged of 20s. on every 336 lb. of kola nuts imported. This article is a most valuable produce, combining the qualities of tea, coffee, and tobacco, and it is the great support and stand-by of the weary traveller, and the porter, staggering under his load, and sweltering in the midday heat, on long and toilsome journeys. The extent of the trade may be judged from the fact that the annual importation is from £30,000 to £35,000 a year into Gambia (in 1883 it was $15\frac{1}{2}$ per cent. of total imports). The produce comes chiefly from the neighbourhood of Sierra Leone, and the trade in this article is almost entirely in the hands of the natives outside the settlement, or, perhaps, the relative high export duty of 5s. the hundredweight would not be charged at that port. This article, the tea and coffee of many natives, is thus made to pay an export duty of £5 a ton at Sierra Leone, and 20s. a ton entrance duty at Gambia. The export trade of Gambia is chiefly with foreign countries ; about 60 per cent. of the exports of 1883 went to France, and $22\frac{1}{2}$ per cent. to England ; the produce is mainly the ground nut, on which there is an export duty of 6s. 8d. a ton. A number of hides are brought from the interior, which are mostly purchased by Americans ; there is an export duty on them of 2d. each. In 1883 about 45 per cent of the imports were British (£41,000 being British cottons and £10,000 in rice), the remainder were from the coast and foreign countries.

Proceeding south to Sierra Leone, the trade with the produce of palm-trees begins to assume large proportions. Out of about £22,000 of palm oil exported in 1883, Great Britain received £14,000, France received nearly all the remainder. The total exports of palm kernels were valued at over

£81,000; France received the largest portion, £31,000, Great Britain came next with £27,000, and Germany took £22,000. All the gum copal, valued at nearly £15,000, went to the United Kingdom. France took nearly all the ground nuts. Of the ginger, 65 per cent. went to the United Kingdom, and nearly all the remainder to the United States, Over £30,000 of kola nuts were shipped to Gambia and Goree. Great Britain received about 38 per cent. of the produce of this settlement, but she sent about 70 per cent. of the imports (£233,000 being in cottons). The United States takes about 7 per cent. of the exports, and sends about 9 per cent. of the imports of this settlement.

Referring to the export duties, this settlement, besides the 5s. per cwt. on kola nuts, charges beny seed 2d. per cwt., ground nuts 3d. per cwt., gum copal 2s. per cwt., palm kernels 2d. per cwt., hides 2d. each, and palm oil 1d. the gallon; as hardly any of the above-mentioned articles exported are the produce of the settlements, and the exported kola nuts are not consumed within the British dominions to which they are exported, these taxes fall on outsiders, and the only question to be determined would be their effect on trade. The kola nut tree grows wild, but is susceptible to cultivation. The produce of the palm oil tree is a pure gift of nature, and the only expense attending it is the collection, preparation, and porterage; the price varies, and the value of palm oil is a good deal influenced by the market for tallow; in fact, the value of African palm oil is largely influenced by the price of Australian tallow. There is no want of competition among the traders on the coast to get it, and it seems as if any quantity would find a market. The palm oil is a chief food of the people, but in that case it is differently and more carefully prepared. It has many advantages, as a food, when fitly prepared, over other oils in common use in Europe, and it might be introduced with advantage. The quantity of palm oil imported into England in 1884 was about 35,200 tons, all of it the produce of West Africa; 39,000 tons of oil nuts were imported in the same year. Africa may well be called the "oilery" of the world.

Sierra Leone is for most articles a free port of entry, the only duty is on kerosene oil, 6d. a gallon, and light duties on beer, ale, spirits, wines, and tobacco (the duty of 6d. per pound weight on common leaf tobacco is much too high, this article is

F

a currency all over that part of Africa, and represents food). Were it not for the policy pursued, already referred to, Freetown would become a great and important trading depôt, and a really great centre for commercial transactions.

The trade of the British Gold Coast is more exclusively with the United Kingdom than that of any other of the British West African settlements. In 1883, out of a total of £382,583 imports, £295,176 were from the United Kingdom, and out of £363,868 exports the United Kingdom received £251,390, of which nearly £168,000 was the produce of the palm oil tree. Germany took about £21,000 in palm tree produce, and the United States nearly £56,000. The United States sent nearly £50,000 in white rum (potato spirit), Great Britain sent £12,000 in gin, mostly of German origin. The cotton goods and haberdashery, &c., valued at about £135,000, were entirely British. The trade of this large settlement is most contemptible in amount, and could easily be £5,000,000 imports with a like value for exports ; but the policy followed has made all trade with the interior practically impossible for the last 30 years or more. Until British authorities make up their minds to come to terms with the powerful inland races, who are among the most intelligent and energetic in Africa, our possessions on this part of the coast will be a real hindrance to any advance among the people. The terms demanded by the people of the interior are, on the whole, just and reasonable, and the coast tribes should be given the alternative of accepting them or being left to themselves. It is the policy of these coast tribes, with which the British Administration has identified itself so long, that has been the fertile cause of all wars and troubles in these parts, and they will certainly be the cause of many more yet to come unless a policy more in accordance with the position of things and the facts to be dealt with be introduced. The British Government can have no right to be in Africa anywhere unless it be there for the general benefit. No one doubts the benefit conferred in some directions, but on a very limited scale, by British administration ; but unless something more be done these advantages can have no real influence on the bulk of the population of the interior.

The duties of customs at the Gold Coast and Lagos are light and simple, being 4 per cent. *ad valorem* on everything except ale, beer, wines, spirits and tobacco—which are specifically but lightly taxed. The duty of 6d. on un-manufactured tobacco is high; the common leaf tobacco in these countries is a chief currency for purposes of barter. What has been said before about the interior people being resentful of the duties levied by the British authorities on the goods in transit to them, applies also to this part of the coast. Some costly British wars have been undertaken here, the real object in dispute being a point on the coast. The natives were determined to have access to it for their trade, and the local British Administration, fearful for its custom houses and its *ad valorem* duties, in fact, for its revenues, were equally determined to keep them off. The British Administration triumphed, of course, but in beating off the natives, the cotton goods of England were to a large extent beaten off also, and excluded from the markets of the interior.

The export trade of Lagos is chiefly in the produce of the palm tree, of which in 1883, £465,000 was exported, out of a total of £594,000 for exports. Great Britain took £107,000 in palm oil and £125,000 in palm kernels; Germany took £128,000 in palm kernels and £47,500 in oil; France took £25,000 in kernels and £27,600 in oil. The United Kingdom sent about 56 per cent. of the imports and took about 44 per cent. of the exports in 1883; but the imports contained articles to the extent of about £20,000 from foreign countries, taken on board in Great Britain; this is one of the parts of Africa, getting fewer every year, where cowries (from Mozambique and Zanzibar), as a currency, are yet dealt in. Nearly all cotton goods are British, the quantity imported in 1883 was valued at over £222,000; nearly £75,000 of Geneva (spirit) was imported, partly from England and partly from Germany, but it was doubtless nearly all of the same German origin. Some of the import and export trade of the port of Lagos is only a coasting trade. Next to Great Britain Germany does the largest trade here; her direct imports in 1883 were £126,000, and her direct exports nearly £177,000.

Lagos, on account of its bar, is not a really good port, but it has water communication with rich countries and among ener-getic races anxious for trade. But the same system being pur-sued here, as elsewhere on the coast under the British flag, the adjoining people are often hostile and always suspicious, and the trade has insignificant proportions to what it might, and easily could, have been made to have.

F 2

There are no export duties at Lagos or the Gold Coast. The customs revenue for these two settlements for the five years 1879–83 came to £664,196, and most of this will have been paid by the interior people—the consumers residing outside British jurisdiction. In some senses it is satisfactory to be thus able to make other people pay for one's administration and government, and it is perhaps the only instance known where duties of customs have this result. Under the circumstances, the moderation in the duties levied should perhaps be commended. People in England, and especially the poor and over-taxed people of continental Europe, know too well that all the customs charges at their ports come out of their own pockets.

The total tonnage of vessels entered at, and cleared from, the British West African ports in the year 1883, was 1,335,398; of this 1,176,293 tons were for steamers, and 1,052,897 tons were under the British flag. As a matter of fact, each steamer calls at every port where there is any cargo to discharge or any produce to be shipped, and this makes the total tonnage to look large. The West African coast is well looked after for cargo, and the vessels belonging to the great companies are always willing to go out of their way to oblige customers, and ship produce from the beach. The contrast is enormous between these parts and the West Indies in this respect, and proves once more the advantage of free competition over heavy Government subsidies.

In Africa the people are fond of their individuality. The land everywhere belongs to the people; the notion of the few holding it and the bulk of the population being their labourers would be repugnant to them. They are what Europeans call savages, and they have slavery among them, but all free men are equal; they cannot understand a free man not being so. They have sound laws which respect what every man possesses; giving honour to position, wealth, and the fruits of industry. In all these countries there are arbitrary acts and cruel despots, but the people prefer these fitful despotisms by their own race to what to them appears a regularly organised, if more humane one, by Europeans. What the people really prefer is to be governed as little as possible by outsiders. They are all very willing to trade, but are distrustful of the ulterior intentions of Europeans.

There is only one policy that could be followed successfully by the British in Western Africa everywhere. It would be a consistent policy. And while it would be in harmony with the greatest traditions of the English people, it would fall completely in with the views, the sentiments, the traditions, the customs, and the habits of the people of the African continent.

The system of native government in Western Africa is usually federal, that is to say, the people are ruled by big councils of native chiefs, where treaties, war and peace, and such matters are determined, and they have lesser councils determining local matters, and family councils settle family questions. Nothing is ever done without a palaver, according to its degree; for if any one acts by his own motion, and does a deed of wrong, or one opposed to the general sentiment, swift and terrible retribution follows. But no council or palaver can upset the proceedings and determinations of any previous council, unless all the contracting parties to the first consent also to the other. This is one of the greatest stumbling-blocks of the local British administrators, who, as a rule, are wholly ignorant of this fact, and they think the decision of every palaver they attend binding, whereas it is only so conditionally. The parties to the second palaver are often accused of being false, when in point of fact they are only true to their constitutional and traditional system; the decisions of the previous palaver not having been abrogated, they are forced to stand by it, even against their will.

The proposed policy is to take advantage of the machinery existing in the land, and honoured and obeyed by the people. Let these great councils that are called together for big palavers be erected into permanent bodies, having complete power over determined areas, such as they now influence, with adequate revenues (say one-tenth of what a direct British administration would cost). The revenues are there, and all the necessary machinery. The British can do this easily; and the certain success and good example of these councils will lead to others being rapidly established on a similar system, and then the interior of the continent will be opened up to commerce and civilisation. The leading missionaries and traders of repute could be joined to these councils, and if necessary a British official would assist the chiefs to lay down rules and regulations.

Nothing in all the history submitted on this subject is more misleading, untrue, and unjust than the reiterated statement

that the chiefs and people of Western Africa are unfitted for
peaceable self-government. It is not pretended they will reach
for the present any Western European ideal, but they will
not lag much behind some people who claim to be better.
The people do not want war ; the very facility with which their
disputes are temporarily adjusted serves to show this disposition.
This coast is far from having recovered from the dire effects of
the slave trade. The chiefs are weak, and much of their
power is taken from them by the very British administration
which scolds them for their non-success. No native power is
ever permitted to levy duties of customs, or other taxes, on the
coast line at all events, but the coast of the country is nevertheless annexed in many places by the British authorities, who
levy taxes and spend the proceeds for purposes unknown to the
natives who pay them.

The present system depends for its very fitful, temporary
and extremely limited success on the active personality of an
Administrator, and when this utmost possible success is
obtained, it is only at the point where the Administrator
happens to be for the moment, and the effect does not outlast
his departure or death. Then the history of British administration on the coast everywhere shows how rare it is to have
an official with the physique and local experience necessary for
even this limited work. It is well known also that this
personal system, at its best, is full of abuses of the worst
kind, politically ; the Administrators, and those who influence
them, get to have favourites, and even chiefs have their
legitimate power, influence, and dignity interfered with, because
they refuse to pay homage to their views. In consequence of
all this, an apparently successful administrator is usually, and
sharply, followed by even worse confusion and more protracted
wars than were known before his advent. It is the history of
all weak, despotic systems, having no basis in the country, or
among the people sought to be governed or influenced.

A policy such as the one sketched above is what is wanted
in those parts where Great Britain has annexed the coast ; it
can be consistent in its acts as in its policy, and will depend
for success, in all its branches, on the people of the country
and their legitimate chiefs. It will inaugurate a real permanent
and progressive government for the people behind the British
possessions where the present systems render all stable government and progress impracticable.

CHAPTER VII.

STRAITS SETTLEMENTS.

THE Straits Settlements, including the adjoining territories under British protection, have not yet been developed to anything like their full capacity for planting purposes. The splendid facilities for trade offered by Singapore, and the profits of mining, have absorbed the energy of those who seek fortunes. All that part of the Malayan Peninsula which is not claimed by Siam is under the dominion of the British Crown by occupation, or as protected territories; both meaning the same thing in practice. In course of time the problems of government in communities such as these will present real difficulties which will no doubt be overcome by the wisdom of the British nation. The population of to-day will not be the population of the future; the movements and amalgamations of races in these parts are among the phenomena of the time; considerable wealth is accumulating in the hands of native merchants, Chinese and others, at the trading ports; education, and a superior civilisation, and social and family life of a higher level than the past, are being rapidly established, and they will bring inevitable changes in the general views and habits of the people. The government and laws will have to conform to all these circumstances in order to render British authority secure, by being founded on mutual interests, and the love and gratitude of the people.

The unchangeable East is changing by its daily and hourly contact with the aggressiveness of the West. Not by the aggressiveness of war, because this has the effect of making people rather cling than otherwise to those old customs and habits which alone conquest and annexation cannot take away from them. The aggressiveness that operates is that of public opinion, of literature, and of commerce; these bring the people into contact with Western thought and habits, and they will adopt them more and more when they see that the complete and definite conquest and annexation they feared are not among the consequences of doing so, but the contrary. It is thus that the leaven of Western civilisation will arouse the people from the slumber of ages. It cannot yet be seen how much of European civilisation and systems the people may elect to adopt, but no one will be able to say to them, this much you may adopt, and no more, and they will demand a preponderating voice in the management of their own concerns. The fear sometimes expressed of the neighbourhood of foreign settlements might be reasonable if Great Britain ever acted unworthily, but if she continues in the paths of justice she need never fear the permanent loss of her legitimate power and just influence among the people. At the same time it is necessary to provide against such places as Singapore being put to ransom, or damaged by an unscrupulous foe.

The population of the four Crown settlements (Singapore, Penang, Malacca, and Wellesley), in 1883, was computed at 3,500 Europeans, 174,000 Chinese, 170,000 Malays, and 41,000 East Indians. The Malays are not likely to increase much— Mohammedan races rarely do so—they are already outnumbered, and before many years are passed they will be only a fraction of the population. The protected territories are also but thinly peopled by Malays; there are a few other inhabitants in remote districts who appear to be the representatives of older races. But the whole peninsula is fated to be ultimately filled up by the Chinese; these people will not be mere labourers and factors for Europeans, they will be landholders, cultivators, and merchants, and if other industries hereafter develop these will also be largely in their hands.

The imports from the United Kingdom for the ten years 1868-77 averaged £2,497,000 a year, and for the six years 1878-83 they were £3,865,000 a year (including bullion and specie, and foreign and colonial produce). This will make the United Kingdom imports for the sixteen years £48,160,000. The exports to the United Kingdom for the same period were valued at £36,645,000. The Board of Trade returns differ from the colonial returns. This is the case with valuations of all colonial imports and exports; but the margin of difference between the two returns varies much. According to the former, the exports to the Straits Settlements, for the sixteen years, were of the value of £36,355,000, and the imports from the Straits Settlements of the value of £50,495,000. This makes the colonial valuation of United Kingdom merchandise and other exports 32½ per cent. higher than the Board of Trade estimates, and the Board of Trade returns give a greater valuation to Straits Settlements' shipments to the United Kingdom by 32 per cent.

The value of British and Irish produce and manufactures alone, exported to the Straits Settlements in the ten years, 1874–83, amounted to £22,502,000 (Board of Trade Returns, at 3s. 8d. = $1). It has been seen the values of goods are differently estimated at the ports of shipment in the United Kingdom from what they usually are on arrival in the colonies; they have naturally, also, a different value at each place. Chief among British goods exported to the Straits Settlements are cottons, wearing apparel, haberdashery, and linens, and woollens; the value of these articles in five years, 1879–83, amounted to £8,207,000 (Board of Trade returns). British coal and fuel (1,312,177 tons) amounted to £689,000. Hardware, cutlery, machinery, metals, and telegraphic necessaries were valued at £1,378,000. The principal articles imported into the United Kingdom from the Straits Settlements in the five years, 1879–1883, were caoutchouc and gutta-percha, £2,850,000; sago and other farinaceous substances, £2,314,000; dye and tanning stuffs, gums, lacs, &c., £2,588,000; pepper and spices, £2,817,000; tin and ores, £4,826,000; and leather and hides, £1,063,000. Sugar amounted to only £916,000, and isinglass to £185,000.

The total imports into the Straits Settlements for the seven years, 1869–75, were valued at £79,361,000; and for the seven years, 1876–83, at £106,187,000. The total exports for the first seven years were valued at £74,184,000, and for the second seven years at £97,436,000. These figures are from colonial returns.

There is a large traffic with the eastern possessions of Holland; during the ten years ending 1883 they shipped to the British Settlements merchandise to the value of £24,210,000, and received through the Settlements to the value of £35,898,000. The direct trade of France, Holland, and Germany with the Settlements figures for £3,891,000 imports, and £6,628,000 exports, in the ten years. There is a large trade with Siam and China, amounting to 15¼ millions sterling imports, and 14½ millions exports, in the ten years, 1874–83. During the same years the imports from Hong-Kong amounted to £16,823,000, and the exports to Hong-Kong to £10,485,000. There was a considerable movement of imports and exports between the several ports of the Malayan Peninsula and Singapore—an inter-colonial and coasting trade of importance. The eastern possessions of France do an important trade;

their imports into the Straits Settlements in the ten years, 1874–83, amounted to £3,677,000, and their exports to £6,763,000; much of this is probably a carrying trade by the French mail steamers (main line), which all touch at Singapore, and have branch lines communicating with French colonial ports. The imports from the eastern possessions of Spain amounted to £1,120,000, and the exports to the same amounted to £1,011,000, in the ten years. There were shipments to the United States averaging for the ten years over £800,000 a year, but no equivalent figures of imports; the total imports from America were only about £600,000 in the five years, 1879–83. The imports from India for the ten years ending 1883, were valued at £24,276,000 (colonial returns), and at £25,890,000 (Indian returns), and the exports to India at £8,355,000 (colonial returns). The Indian returns always include imports and exports for Government account. The trade of the Settlements with Independent Borneo and Sarawak for the ten years, 1874–83, averaged £138,000 a year imports, and £104,000 a year exports. The trade with Labuan averaged £62,020 a year imports, and £29,000 a year exports, during the same period. The chief trade of these Settlements is with the United Kingdom, Hong-Kong, the Dutch possessions, Siam, China, India, and between their own ports and the Malayan Peninsula.

In the five years, 1879–83, the Dutch East India possessions, besides the trade done *viâ* Singapore, imported from the United Kingdom merchandise, the produce and manufacture of the United Kingdom, to the value of £9,344,000, of which £7,108,000 were cottons, linens, and woollens; they exported to the United Kingdom produce valued at £14,518,000, of which £14,002,000 was sugar. It will be seen above that these colonies of Holland, in the trade with Singapore, received £11,688,000 more in merchandise than they shipped to that port; much of this balance will be in payment of the balance due on the sugar, in the shape of British goods. The great free ports of Singapore and Hong-Kong give British merchants many facilities for trading in Eastern seas. During the five years, 1879–83, British goods, the produce and manufacture of the United Kingdom, valued at £5,909,000, were sent to the Philippine Islands, of which £4,376,000 were cottons, linens, woollens, and apparel. Great Britain received £9,491,000 in produce, of which £5,700,000 was in sugar, and £3,332,000 in hemp. The trade of the United Kingdom with Siam, Cochin China, and Borneo is chiefly transacted through Singapore.

Labuan is a settlement that at one time promised much, from its possession of valuable coal deposits, its position and fine harbour. It acts as an intermediate station between Singapore and the large island of Borneo; some of the produce of the latter is prepared at Labuan for the Singapore market. When the Duke of Buckingham and Chandos was Secretary of State for the Colonies (1868), with Sir C. B. Adderley (since Lord Norton) as Parliamentary Under-Secretary, it was proposed to incorporate this island with the Straits Settlements; unfortunately for Labuan the recommendations then formulated were not carried through. Labuan has lately been annexed to the British North Borneo Company; not formally, it is true, but practically. It is to be hoped its inhabitants as well as those of North Borneo will never have cause to believe the British flag may be indirectly employed to cover any acts different in character and in principle from those which have made its chief renown among the oppressed.

There are other places in the world besides Singapore which would show similar results, in proportion to possible commerce, had they the same advantages of absolute free trade. But for the purpose of obtaining the little or great revenue necessary for local purposes of administration, imports and commerce are taxed, and the stream of wealth passes their ports and seeks other lands.

The revenue of this colony for purposes of government are raised chiefly by a monopoly of the preparation for use of rough opium from India, and the farming out of the privilege to sell opium preparations and spirits. There are spirit, opium, and toddy farmers, and licences for pawnbrokers, hotels, and such like. Land brings in a revenue from its sale and from rents and fees, but much of it, it appears, was alienated in fee simple before the year 1871. In Singapore land is usually held direct from the Crown by lease or grant for a long term of years. In the country, pepper and gambier plantations have sometimes 10 years' leases. Quit rents for country land are now from 40 cents of a dollar per acre—readjustable every 30 years. The same system obtains at Penang and Malacca, but native customary tenure without written evidence of title is accepted. Unoccupied Crown lands may be had on lease for 999 years on payment of the quit rent and a premium. Permits are granted to hold land in anticipation of the survey, and much is so held in Province Wellesley. The actual conditions of tenure seem to vary much—according to what happened to be the policy at the time the agreements were made. It is said there are 18 different forms of title in the hands of the Singapore public, and 20 in the hands of the inhabitants of Penang. To interfere with past arrangements would be impolitic and dangerous. If the people are satisfied there can be no reasons to change or simplify existing methods. But in some countries such a condition of things would give plenty of work to the lawyers. There are stamp duties and the usual fees and fines of Court and the Post Office. Port dues are only 3 cents the registered ton. With these taxes and some few unimportant items a revenue for the purposes of government has been raised without pressure or difficulty. The revenue for the 3 years ending 1879 averaged about £373,000 a year, for the 3 years ending 1882 the average was £469,000 a year, in 1883 it was £559,000. A large proportion of this revenue is spent on public works. The rapid augmentation of a revenue that does not press on industry need not be regarded with suspicion, if it be spent advantageously.

In the year 1884 the craft that entered Singapore numbered 15,265, with 300,472 people for crews; 4,551 were British vessels, measuring 2,467,739 tons, and with 166,252 crews; 9,417 were native vessels, measuring 266,594 tons, with crews numbering 70,732; there were 1,291 foreign vessels with crews numbering 63,488.

The advantages of a free trade policy are too apparent at a place like Singapore to need dwelling on. People are apt to ascribe all the prosperity to the special position and natural advantages of the place. Of course these advantages do exist, but there are numerous other places, as a glance at a map will show, equally well placed and having similar advantages, but where a restrictive policy has made all progress impossible. Even vast numbers of small and frail native craft from distant islands, some two or three thousand miles away, through weary weeks and months of a toilsome navigation, laboriously seek Singapore, passing Dutch and other ports innumerable—places in other respects more suitable and nearer for them—whose restrictive systems repulse trade and make even these people prefer the more distant free port of Singapore, where they can trade and traffic as they please.

CHAPTER VIII.

HONG KONG.

HONG KONG is in many ways the ideal of what a port should be. It owes much to locality and to its capacity, but its pre-eminent position is due to its being a free port under the British flag. As in most places in the world where powerful interests have much at stake, abuses crept in, and some sections of the community got to be favoured, and others, equally entitled to respect and consideration, had to struggle against injustice and adverse conditions. Most, if not all, of these objections have been removed, and the local laws and regulations show no blots, or only a few, in this respect. Every nationality in the world claiming to do foreign trade with the East is represented here. Englishmen might well be proud to see what may be done under their flag when the great national principles of free trade are given full scope, and commerce, untrammelled by vexatious regulations, is allowed to grow and develop in its might.

The colony gives no returns of imports and exports, that being impracticable; but it is the chief centre, and, as it were, the focus of the trade of China and Japan with the West. The Board of Trade returns show that it imported from the United Kingdom, in the five years 1879–83, merchandise valued at £17,087,000, of which £16,264,000 were manufactured goods and produce of Great Britain and Ireland, £13,257,000 being apparel, cottons, linens, and woollens. The imports into the United Kingdom from Hong Kong consist of portions of the produce of China, Japan, and other Eastern countries, which it was found most convenient to send through that port, and also the above merchandise shipped to Hong Kong direct from the United Kingdom was only a portion of the goods intended for such countries, the remainder being shipped to them direct. Hong Kong received from Great Britain 365,000 tons of coal and fuel in five years, 1879–83; but she also obtains large supplies of these articles from other countries, some of which are nearer and more handy than England.

The revenue of the colony averaged about £244,000 a year for the five years 1879–83. The revenue for 1884 was $1,171,099 ($118,350 less than the previous year); at 4s. 2d. a dollar, this is £243,977. The population in 1883 numbered 7,990 whites, 1,722 coloured, and 150,690 Chinese; total, 160,402. The taxation is, therefore, $7·31 per head. For such a rich port this compares favourably with the taxation per head in the poor, ill-taxed agricultural settlements. The reve-nue is raised by rents on Crown lands put up to auction for terms of years; by rents on stone quarries, and market charges; by spirit licences, and licences to sell and prepare opium, and by market charges. There are the usual stamps, court fees, &c. There are taxes on houses for lighting and police pur-poses, and there are port charges.

Chinamen live cheaply almost anywhere; they probably can do so effectively in this great port. Predial labour is paid in kind, and ordinary labour is about 17 cents of a dollar a day. Skilled and mechanical labour is proportionately paid higher, but it is not dear.

In the year 1884 the number of vessels that entered Hong Kong harbour was 26,763, measuring 5,167,231 tons, and hav-ing 431,429 people as crews. Among these were 23,473 Chinese junks, of 1,687,594 tons, with 290,846 crews. There were 2,397 vessels under the British flag, measuring 2,685,194 tons, and having 106,364 crews. The next in importance are the Germans, with 474 vessels, 309,171 tons, 10,389 crews. The Americans come next with 146 vessels, 192,803 tons, and 5,797 men (the Americans have always fewer hands on their commercial—especially sailing—vessels than other people). The French have 104 vessels, 156,120 tons, and 20,346 men. Out of the total number of British vessels it seems that only 148 arrived direct from the United Kingdom. The movements of commerce are most complicated, but the study is deeply inter-esting, and of great moment for a commercial people. The rise of such ports as Hong Kong and Singapore are only possi-ble on free trade principles. Although all the great powers of the world, as may be seen, are interested in these ports, and do much of their Eastern trade through them, every friend of free-dom must be fearful to see them so insecure as to be open to a passing raid, and the heavy attendant losses, by any enter-prising ironclad.

CHAPTER IX.

FALKLAND ISLANDS, ST. HELENA, GIBRALTAR, BERMUDA.

THE above Crown colonies have each a special interest and value. The Falkland Islands are a colony that will be of much importance hereafter to the Empire. In the present redundance of available colonies for Europeans, the perplexed emigrant hardly knows which to select. There are so many that are more accessible, and present more attractive features, that it will be yet some time before these distant and breezy islands will be in request. A population of 1,600 souls to an area of 6,500 square miles is not much; but they manage to send to England produce of their own of an annual average value of £53 per head, of which £42 per head is in sheep and lambs' wool. Almost all the export trade is direct with the United Kingdom. The only customs' charges are 2s. per lb. on tobacco, and 4s. per lb. on cigars, 3d. a gallon on ale in wood, and 6d. a dozen in bottles, wine 2s. a gallon in wood, and 4s. a dozen in bottles, and spirits 10s. a gallon.

St. Helena has lately had to live a good deal on the memory of the past. The Suez Canal took from it its main importance. All the whale fishing in the Indian Ocean and south of it is in the hands of Americans, whose vessels are able to fit out and provision cheaply for a three or four years' stay; and these make St. Helena one of their stations to refit, and to stow and forward their oil. The days of St. Helena are, nevertheless, not gone for ever, From its position it need fear no rivals. The western coast of Africa is developing rapidly, and, by-and-by, more powerful, larger, and faster vessels than are now dreamt of will again seek the route to the East, *via* the Cape. St: Helena will find itself again a much needed position. The only duties of customs charged here are, for ale in the wood $4\frac{1}{2}$d. a gallon, and 1s. per dozen bottles, wine in the wood 2s. 6d. a gallon and 5s. per dozen bottles, leaf tobacco 6d. per lb., manufactured tobacco and cigars 1s. per lb.

Bermuda is chiefly noted as a naval and military port; it is sometimes regarded as geographically one of the West India Islands, but it has little in common with these groups, except that the population, to some extent, is composed of African races and their descendants. The revenue is about £30,000 a year, four-fifths of which is raised by custom-house charges. These charges are, nevertheless, not high. Ale pays 4½d. a gallon in wood and 1s. a dozen bottles, wine pays 20 per cent. *ad valorem*, all tobaccos pay 2d. per pound and cigars 10s. the 1,000, spirits 4s. gallon, coal and books are free, everything else pays 5 per cent. *ad valorem.* The average yearly imports into the island for the 10 years 1874–83 were valued in the colony at about £254,000, and the average yearly exports for the same period at about £80,000. Much of the imports will be for the use of the garrison. Only about £55,000 a year of the imports are in British goods, £11,000 a year being for ale and beer.

Gibraltar is classed as a Crown colony, but practically it is a British stronghold under a purely military administration. The population in 1881 (exclusive of military) was reckoned to be 18,381. The yearly revenue varies between £44,000 and £49,000 a year, of which about £10,000 is from duties of customs, the remainder being obtained by land rents, port dues and fees, &c. The exports to the United Kingdom are unimportant ; but the imports of the produce and manufacture of the United Kingdom are considerable, chiefly for sale to passing vessels and for garrison supplies. In the 5 years 1879–83 they amounted to £3,629,000, of which £1,580,000 was for wearing apparel, cottons, linens, and woollens, £245,000 for beer and ale, and £183,000 for refined sugar. The imports also included 1,817,000 tons of British coal, valued at £911,000. In 1883 vessels of all nations, measuring 9,504,093 tons entered and cleared, of which 7,602,423 tons were under British colours, and 9,256,703 tons of the whole were steamers.

Printed by Cassell & Co., Limited, La Belle Sauvage, Ludgate Hill, E.C.

History of the Free Trade Movement in England. *Fifth Edition.* By AUGUSTUS MONGREDIEN, Author of "Free Trade and English Commerce." Price *1s.*

The Land Question. Its Examination and Solution from an Agricultural point of View. By THOMAS J. ELLIOT, M.R.A.C. *10s. 6d.*

Italy: from the Fall of Napoleon I. in 1815 to the Death of Victor Emmanuel (of Savoy), First King of United Italy, in 1878. By JOHN WEBB PROBYN. Demy 8vo, cloth, *7s. 6d.*

The Coming Struggle for India. By Prof. ARMINIUS VAMBÉRY. Extra crown 8vo, cloth, *5s.*
** In this new work the author describes the various countries and peoples conquered by Russia in her successive advances towards India, and details her intrigues in Afghanistan. The work shows the influence which has been exerted by Russian rule in the territories conquered by the soldiers of the Czar, contrasting it with the effect produced by the British régime in India.

India: the Land and the People. By SIR JAMES CAIRD, K.C.B., F.R.S. *Revised and Enlarged Edition.* Demy 8vo, cloth, with Map, *10s. 6d.*
The Right Hon. John Bright says:—"I have read this book through carefully, and with much interest and pleasure. It differs from other books on India, and gives, I think, a better idea of the state of the country and the condition of the people than I have found elsewhere."

Life and Labour in the Far, Far West. By W. HENRY BARNEBY. With Map of Author's Route, *16s.*

Bright, John, Life and Times of the Rt. Hon. By W. ROBERTSON. 608 pages. With Etching from the Portrait by W. W. OULESS, R.A. *7s. 6d.*

Gladstone, Life of the Right Hon. W. E. By GEORGE BARNETT SMITH. With Steel Portrait. Revised to Summer of 1883. Price *3s. 6d.* Jubilee Edition, with Portrait, *1s.*
"The most comprehensive and satisfactory Life of Mr. Gladstone which has yet been given to the public."—*Edinburgh Daily Review.*

A History of Modern Europe. By C. A. FYFFE, M.A. Vol. I. From the Outbreak of the Revolutionary War in 1792 to the Accession of Louis XVIII. in 1814. Price *12s.*

Russia. By D. MACKENZIE WALLACE, M.A. *New and Cheaper Edition*, in One Vol., demy 8vo, with Coloured Maps, cloth, *5s.* "A delightful book, instructive and attractive."—*Scotsman.*

Working Men Co-operators: What they have Done, and What they are Doing. By ARTHUR H. DYKE ACLAND and BENJAMIN JONES. *1s.*

WORKS PUBLISHED FOR THE COBDEN CLUB

By CASSELL & COMPANY, Limited.

Local Government and Taxation in the United Kingdom. With Contributions by the Hon. G. C. BRODRICK, C. T. D. ACLAND, M.P., LORD EDMOND FITZMAURICE, M.P., &c. &c. Edited by J. W. PROBYN. Cloth, price 5s.

A Primer of Tariff Reform. By DAVID A. WELLS (U.S. America). Price 6d.

The Reform of the English Land System. By the Hon. GEORGE C. BRODRICK, Warden of Merton College, Oxford, Author of "English Land and English Landlords." Price 3d.

The Three Panics. An Historical Episode. By RICHARD COBDEN. Price 1s.

Free Trade versus Fair Trade. By Sir T. H. FARRER, Bart., Secretary to the Board of Trade. Price 2s. 6d.

Free Trade and English Commerce. By AUGUSTUS MONGREDIEN. New and Revised Edition, 6d.

England under Free Trade. By G. W. MEDLEY. Price 3d.

Pleas for Protection Examined. By AUGUSTUS MONGREDIEN. Price 6d.

Popular Fallacies regarding Trade and Foreign Duties: Being the "SOPHISMES ÉCONOMIQUES" of FRÉDÉRIC BASTIAT. Adapted to the Present Time by E. R. PEARCE-EDGCUMBE. Price 6d.

The Reciprocity Craze: A Tract for the Times. By GEORGE W. MEDLEY. Price 3d.

Depression in the West Indies: Free Trade the only Remedy. By C. S. SALMON. Price 6d.

Western Farmer of America. By AUGUSTUS MONGREDIEN. Price 3d.

Our Land Laws of the Past. By the Right Hon. W. E. BAXTER, M.P. Price 3d.

The Transfer of Land by Registration under the Duplicate Method operative in British Colonies. By Sir ROBERT TORRENS, K.C.M.G. Price 6d.

PRINTED BY CASSELL & COMPANY, LIMITED, LA BELLE SAUVAGE, LONDON, E.C.

Ingram Content Group UK Ltd.
Milton Keynes UK
UKHW030919080323
418175UK00010B/706